POETRY COMP

GREAT MINDS

Your World...Your Future...YOUR WORDS

From Lancashire
Edited by Jessica Woodbridge

 Young**Writers**

First published in Great Britain in 2005 by:
Young Writers
Remus House
Coltsfoot Drive
Peterborough
PE2 9JX
Telephone: 01733 890066
Website: www.youngwriters.co.uk

All Rights Reserved

© Copyright Contributors 2005

SB ISBN 1 84460 703 8

Foreword

This year, the Young Writers' 'Great Minds' competition proudly presents a showcase of the best poetic talent selected from over 40,000 up-and-coming writers nationwide.

Young Writers was established in 1991 to promote the reading and writing of poetry within schools and to the youth of today. Our books nurture and inspire confidence in the ability of young writers and provide a snapshot of poems written in schools and at home by budding poets of the future.

The thought, effort, imagination and hard work put into each poem impressed us all and the task of selecting poems was a difficult but nevertheless enjoyable experience.

We hope you are as pleased as we are with the final selection and that you and your family continue to be entertained with *Great Minds From Lancashire* for many years to come.

Contents

Rachael Williams (14)	26
Neela Dookhun (14)	27
Naomi Atkinson (14)	28
Chloe Anderton (14)	29
Hannah Almond (14)	30
Amy McDowell (14)	31
Tom Kirby (15)	32
Anna Gelasia Sheasby (14)	33
Yasmin Mogra (14)	34
Oliver Malcolm-Gregson (11)	34
Keira Gilchrist (14)	35
Charlotte McKee (14)	36
Helen-Ema Calvert (12)	37
Lizzie Parsons (14)	38
Abigail Green (12)	39
Naomi Saint (12)	40
Janet Barton (14)	41
Lucy Crook (14)	42
Amber Watson (14)	43
Elliott Park (14)	44
Chris Glover (12)	45
Victor Chow (12)	46
Vicki Holden (14)	47
Danni Harrison (14)	48
Sam Hughes (11)	49
Joanne Cottam (14)	50
Luke Jenner (13)	51
Hannah Wright (12)	52
Daniel McCormick (14)	53
Elizabeth Johnston (12)	54
Jordan Thompson (11)	55
Abbi Hough (12)	56
Grace Xia (12)	57
Rowena Astin (12)	58
Sam McGrievy-Smith (12)	59
Beth Horsley (12)	60
Charlotte Feeny (11)	61
David Robinson (12)	62
Nicola Wilson (12)	63
Grace Conlon (11)	64
Andrew Johnson (12)	65
Nicola Doolan (13)	66

Sarah Fisher (11)	67
Lauren Chapman (11)	68
Mary Clayton (12)	69
Emma Worthington (11)	70
Martha Smith (11)	71
Robert Newton (11)	72
Sima Patel (12)	73
Almajane Blaylock (11)	74
Priya Modasiya (11)	75
Kristian Hensby (11)	76

Brookfield School

Joshua Rothwell (13)	76
Josh Danson (14)	77
Robert Oakley (13)	78
Cameron Leyland (13)	78
Stefan Smith (15)	79
Grant Whillans (14)	79
Anthony Lesley (13)	80
Shea Holloway (12)	80
Steven Macaskill (14)	81

Colne Primet High School

Josh Knapton (12)	81
Rebecca Whitaker (12)	82
Sally Wilkinson (12)	82
Tahrina Golding (12)	83
David Fishwick (11)	83
Jade Tattersall (12)	84
Henna Murad (12)	84
Toni Dey (12)	85
James Smith (11)	85
Mark Brennan (12)	86
Jamie Harvey (12)	87
Rebecca Thompson (11)	88
Naomi Coultas Ferns (11)	88
Byford Adlington (11)	88
Abigail Hirst (11)	89
Freddie Bailey (12)	89
Sophie Holdsworth (11)	89
Josh Hindle (13)	90

Ashleigh Lonsdale (11)	90
Shaun Mullens (12)	91
Toqir Hussain (12)	91
Sabrina Rahman (12)	92
Lauren Kegg (12)	92
Suzanne O'Brien (12)	93
Charlotte Connell (11)	93
Siân Simpson (13)	94
Simon Thornton (11)	94
Chlôe Jane Savage (12)	95
Andrew King (11)	95
Waris Ali (12)	96
Jamie Ingram (11)	96
Arooj Butt (12)	97
Sonia Rahman (11)	97
Chris Willett (12)	98
Umar Waqar (13)	99
Bethany Golding (13)	100
Alex Evans-Shaw (12)	101
Robert Thompson (12)	102
Sigourney Millward (12)	103
Charlotte Stone	104
Warren Singleton (13)	104
Billy Warren (12)	105
Keely Ashworth (12)	105
Matthew Brooks (13)	106
Natalie Whitfield (12)	106
James Hirst (13)	107
Kyle Pearson (12)	107
Daniel West (12)	108
Kayli Morant (13)	109
Charlotte Branch (13)	110
Katy Martin (12)	111
Salma Hussain (13)	112
Daisy Eve (13)	113
Shane Goodwin (12)	114

George Tomlinson School

Cameron Biggar	114
Misbah Javed (12)	115
Emily McDaid (12)	115

Hornby High School

Sarah Newsham (15)	132
Madeleine Larmour (13)	132
Hannah Greene (11)	133
Rebecca Mackay (11)	133
John Dean Elsworth (11)	134
Laura Hearsey (11)	135
Lorelle Bell (13)	136
Victoria Parker (13)	136
Samantha Jordan (13)	137
Laura McKeown (14)	137
Abigail Atkin (12)	137
Annemarie Stevens (13)	138
Amy Graham (13)	138
Ryan Oldfield (12)	139
Bethany Gill (11)	139
Tom Harris (12)	140
Hanna Sill (12)	140
Arthur Lankester (11)	141
Leanne Ashcroft (12)	141
Theodor Ensbury (12)	141
Nicole Keeping (11)	142
Daniel Larmour (12)	142

Leyland St Mary's RC Technology College

Jay Minuti (12)	143
Laura Bolton (13)	143
DJ Beswick (12)	144
Christopher Coulson (12)	144
Megan Walters (12)	145
Cecilia Brown (12)	146
Victoria Butler (12)	147
Dominique Harrison-Bentzen (12)	148
Jessica Illsley (12)	148
Louise Hendy (12)	149

Little Lever School (Specialist Language College)

Marcus Webb (14)	149
Jamie Gordon (15)	150
Alexander Clarkson (13)	150
Catherine Doyle (14)	151

Our Lady's Catholic College

Leah Kelly (12)	173
Zoë Cannar (11)	173
Hannah Webster (11)	174
Leah Bradford (11)	175
Peter Townsend (11)	175
Abigail Gray (11)	176
Megan McCallum (11)	176
Lucy Tomlinson (12)	177

Ripley St Thomas CE High School

Rachel Bates (11)	177
Loren Kyles-Ashton (11)	178
Sophie Wilson (11)	178
Oliver McNamara (14)	179
Emily Stocks (11)	179
Faye Cameron (13)	180
William Hunt (11)	180
Olivia Jamin (12)	181
Charlotte Brown (12)	181
Hannah Jackson (11)	182
Owen Dunne (11)	183
Kate Corfield (12)	184
Heather Cross (14)	185
Peter Kneale (13)	186
Stephanie Wood (11)	186
Simon Saunders (11)	187
Andrew Drummond (12)	187
Oliver David Bray (15)	188
Hannah Jackson & Loren Kyles-Ashton (11)	188
Emily Inston (13)	189
James Birchall (14)	189
Ricky Cusimano (11)	190
Emily Casey (13)	191
Rachel Roberts (11)	192
Farrah Boutros (11)	192
Rosanna Wood (11)	193
Joe Higginson (12)	193
Jessica Stainer (14)	194
Emma Brzezinka (11)	194
Emma Gardner (14)	195

Josh Smith (13)	196
Ross Jesmont (13)	196
Lizzy Wilkinson (13)	197
Emily Greenhalgh (13)	197
Rebecca Marwood (14)	198
Emma Barton (13)	199
Amy Westworth (13)	200
Charlotte Philipson (13)	200
Lewis Cockerill (13)	201
Christina Wren (13)	201
Jane Salisbury (13)	202
Rupert Callingham (13)	203
Peter Smyth (13)	203
Jemma Smith (14)	204
Alexandra Bolsover (13)	204
Jenna Holden (13)	205
Emily Dow (13)	205
Faith Donaldson (14)	206
Stephen Tagg (13)	207
Lucy Stevenson (13)	208
Jane Harrison (14)	208
Victoria Peill (14)	209
Lucy Hobbs (14)	209
Heather Park (14)	210
Matthew Liu (14)	211
Lucy Gager (14)	212
Josh Atkinson (14)	212
Claire Caskie (14)	213
Thomas Fleetwood (14)	213
Jack Ireland (14)	214
Catherine Lund (14)	214
Jess Archer (14)	215
Alex Johnson (14)	215
Isabel Burnside (14)	216

Rivington & Blackrod High School

Hannah Fletcher (13)	216
Ryan Harrison (14)	217
Rebecca Hannell (13)	217

Stonyhurst College

Tom O'Donnell (14)	218
William O'Byrne (14)	218
Jack Wood (13)	219
Edward Johnson (13)	219
Nicola Agius (16)	220
Charlie Fogden (13)	220
Frances Warner (14)	221
Hugh Holt (13)	221
Austin Culley (14)	222
Amy Townsend (14)	222
Vicky McNeill (14)	223
Gertrude Okello (14)	223
Marco Moreno (15)	224
Bob Townsend (15)	224
Patrick McFarlane (15)	225
Todd Robinson (13)	225
Onajite Emerhor (13)	226
Anthony Satterthwaite (14)	227
Joshua McAllister (14)	228
Matthew Richardson (15)	229
Adrian Riley (14)	230
James Kennedy (15)	230
Rosanna Martin (14)	231
Chuba Nwokedi (14)	231
Alexander Ewart (15)	232
Luke Robinson (14)	232
Daniel Church-Taylor (13)	233
Chris Fitzgerald (14)	233
Edward Medwecki (15)	234
Benedict Burgess (15)	235
Jack McGovern (15)	236
Sam Reed (13)	236
Molly Aylward (13)	237
Isabel Howat (16)	238
Dan Layzell (14)	238
Joseph Curry (15)	239
Emily Mullen (13)	240
Scarlett Thompson (16)	240

The Poems

The Subaru

The shiny blue body glints in the sun,
As it revs further to the bass of the drum.

The boot shakes with the roar of the exhaust,
Which sounds something like an angry ghost.

The spoiler itself is as big as a tree,
But the car is as beautiful as can be.

It could beat Kelly Holmes,
Although it's as fat as Aunt Marge, and as long as a horse.

The twinkling gold alloys shimmer in the moonlight,
They are 19" alloys and the best time to see them is at night.

When the bright purple neons light up,
If you saw them, you'd probably drop your cup.

Are you imagining this desirable blue car?
Well it's not so far
I'll tell you what
It's my dad's car!

Trishna Modessa (11)
Archbishop Temple School

Christmas Poem

People go out and sing,
Money for the diamond ring.
People decorate their house,
I just play with my mouse.

I can decorate my Christmas tree,
But then I'll wait for my Christmas tea.
I will look out my bedroom window, looking at the stars,
Then all of a sudden I will count the cars.

I will wait for Santa to come,
But then I'll suck my thumb.
I will have my Christmas pudding,
Then I'll go out clubbing.

Megan Brindle (12)
Archbishop Temple School

Cars

The body is sleek and smooth,
Hot rubber tyres grinding on the move.
Silver paintwork gleaming in the sun,
Swerving round corners having fun.

Speeding on the highway like a river flowing gently,
The engine is roaring like a Bentley.
Everything seems so slow
And cars are moving beside me like a river flow.

The steering wheel big and round,
Putting the brakes on like a pound.
Gear shifts quick and swift,
Putting down the accelerator to get a lift.

Going round corners sharp and fast,
Hit the straight and we're a blast.
End of the road, brakes on,
Nearly there and out gets Don.

Speeding at 180,
People are getting scared matey.
Drop down to 60
And the car goes swiftly.

The fun is over
And now we're going to Dover.
Time to eat
And get with the beat.

Chethan Chauhan (13)
Archbishop Temple School

My Perfect Pony

As it galloped through the pure white snow,
Its hooves crisping through the crispy ground,
He could not go on, but his stamina told him to go,
It was silent, there was no sound, was he ever going to be found?

Its body as white as could be,
It looked so elegant as everyone could see,
It did not look so wild and free,
When I came closer it did not flee.

Its eyes as blue as the sky,
As it stared at me I felt safe,
I knew I would have to say bye,
I knew he had some faith.

As I walked away he followed me,
I felt so tight,
I wanted him to gallop away and be free,
However I knew I was right.

As I walked back to him, he came to me,
I would never leave him on his own,
I knew he was to be,
I never wanted him to be alone.

So I rode him back home,
Now he can stay with me,
Therefore he will never be alone,
Now he is with me so he is not wild and free.

Now he can stay with me!
I can ride him and we can both be free!

Rebecca Haworth (13)
Archbishop Temple School

Christmas Time!

Christmas is the best time of year,
Turkey, spuds, wine and beer.
Everyone has a lot of fun,
On Boxing Day everyone weighs a tonne.
Eating and drinking all of the night,
The kids, they're all as high as a kite.
The Christmas tree is all trimmed and lit up,
Where Santa has been, there is a trace of soot.
Children open up their presents and sweets,
Giving their pets some Christmas treats.
Snowmen, scarves and woolly hats,
Fireplaces covered up by the snuggled up cats.
Teenagers and toddlers, sledging and sleighing,
Children and babies, laughing and playing.
Cards and tinsel upon the wall,
Relatives are shouting, 'Happy Christmas to you all.'
When Christmas is over everyone can't wait
Until next year, it will be so great.

Jordan Blakeley (13)
Archbishop Temple School

Snowman

Snow is fun,
Snow is great,
Something nobody can hate.
All the children in the snow,
Making snowmen, here we go.
The snow is falling all around,
All the children laugh out loud.
People gather in a crowd,
They stare at the snowman
That stands tall and proud.

Craig West (13)
Archbishop Temple School

Christmas

Snow is falling on the ground,
In the streets there is no sound.
Cars, lamp posts and gardens white,
All this snow came last night.

On the tree are sparkly lights,
Twinkle, twinkle, shining bright.
Presents spread out on the chairs,
Christmas stockings on the stairs.

Christmas dinner on the table,
Pull a cracker and read the label.
Children opening all their gifts,
Parents been working extra shifts.

Tinsel on the Christmas tree,
Everyone's merry and very happy.
Hats, gloves, scarves and coats,
Making snow angels with halos that float.

Fiona Chester (13)
Archbishop Temple School

Rainbow

Red is the first,
The colour of Santa.
Then comes yellow,
A fluffy marshmallow.
Here is pink,
The colour to make you think.
Next is green,
An ugly, jealous queen.
Along comes purple,
In the Quality Street.
Soon is orange,
Like the Tango man.
Last in the queue,
It has to be blue.

Matthew Wilcox (13)
Archbishop Temple School

My Usual Boring Day

I wake up in the morning
Already yawning
As I head off to school.

Another boring day at school
Yet all I want is to be cool
As I head to lunch.

I finally get some food
With my favourite dude
As I head off to lessons.

Why am I in French?
All I want is to sit on a bench
As I head home.

Next I have to do my homework
As my brothers lurk
As I head to the table.

I have my tea
Like it used to be
As I head to my mum.

There's my mum
She is like a maid, never a scum
As I head to bed.

I fall asleep
As I get ready for the next day.

Daniel Holyfield (12)
Archbishop Temple School

Black!

Black is midnight,
Pitch-black, frosty night,
Twinkling stars,
The moon above your head.

Black is the witch's cat,
It's bad luck when you pass one,
It's their eyes that stick in your mind,
Their claws sharp and long.

Black is death,
Eyes blackened,
Funerals shrouded,
People saddened.

Black is sweets,
Liquorice Allsorts,
Sweet treacle toffee
On Bonfire Night.

Black is smoke
On Bonfire Night,
Swirls of flames,
Black, thick smoke.

Black is hair,
Long, short, curly hair,
Pigtails stick out
With electrical shocks.

Emma Baines (12)
Archbishop Temple School

Friendship

A friend is someone who is kind,
A friend is someone who doesn't mind,
A friend is someone who always shares,
A friend is someone who always cares.

A friend is a person who is a star,
A friend is a person who won't go far,
Friends are people who always stay together,
Friends are people who will come out whatever the weather.

Friends are people who are never cruel,
A friend is someone who will never act like a fool,
Friends are people who are always up for a laugh,
Friends are people who will care for you down life's path.

Friends are people who never frown
And will always care for you when you're feeling down,
Friends will always bring good cheer
And keep you going through the year.

Friends, friends, friends are true,
Friends will always help you through,
Friends will always be there whatever you do
And also when you're feeling blue.

So keep your friends close and true
And never forget that they love you.

George Buck (12)
Archbishop Temple School

Pink

Pink is soft as snow,
Pink is suited for a baby pink bow,
Pink is as pink as the petals on a rose,
Pink is strawberry ice cream on a cone,
      Pink, pink,
      Pink, pink,
      Pink, pink.
Pink is as cuddly as a new fluffy teddy,
Pink is as sweet as a little baby's boots,
Pink is as cute as a little girl's room,
Pink is as colourful as a bonfire spark!
Pink is as cuddly as a new baby's toy,
      Pink, pink,
      Pink, pink,
      Pink, pink.
Pink is the colour of the sky at night,
Pink is as pink as a pink feather boa,
Pink is as beautiful as a new flower blooming,
Pink is candyfloss, rock and candy.
      Pink, pink,
      Pink, pink,
      Pink, pink.
Light pink, dark pink, fluorescent pink, baby pink,
Pink is my favourite colour, do you like pink?
      Pink, pink,
      Pink, pink,
      Pink!

Chloe Fisher (12)
Archbishop Temple School

Red

What is red?
Red is fire
Burning throughout the night.
Red is blood
Dripping from a fresh cut.

What is red?
Red is anger
Raging to get out.
Red is heat
Keeping us warm.

What is red?
Red looks like roses,
Flowers for love.
Red tastes like fire
Burning in your mouth.

What is red?
Red is embarrassment
Making your face glow.

Sam Griffin (12)
Archbishop Temple School

Rainbow

Red is fire,
Orange is a setting sun,
Yellow is bright like a street lamp
Shining in the night.

Green is grass on a summer's day,
Butterflies fluttering in the blue haze,
Deepest indigo after the sun sets,
As violet shadows creep across the sky.

Thomas Kenworthy (12)
Archbishop Temple School

Christmas Time

Christmas, Christmas what a beautiful time,
All about celebrations with gifts, drinks and wine.
Christmas comes only once a year,
A chance for adults to drink beer.
A time for giving and also sharing,
A time for loving and also caring.
All the snow makes it all fun
And shows the winter has just begun.

I see all the gifts laid under the tree
And I wonder what is there for me?
We leave the milk and cookies on the side,
But Santa waits and hides.
We stay up all night
Waiting for Santa to give us a fright.
As the morning comes I rise with joy
As I can see my great big toy.

Stuart Teague (13)
Archbishop Temple School

Tornado!

Twisting, turning,
Black as night,
Whipping the land,
An awful sight.

Smothering towns,
Devouring fields,
Taking big bites,
Of a monstrous meal.

Leaving the land,
All beaten and bare,
The awful beast
Returns to its lair.

Raegen Gilchrist (12)
Archbishop Temple School

Black

Black is like the night sky,
Black is a dark alley or a dark cave,
Black is an ink spillage.

Black tastes like liquorice,
Black feels like tarmac on a road,
Black is bats hanging from a tree,
Black is a dark place with shining torches.

Black is a small closet,
Black is time to go to sleep,
Black is when you turn the lights off.

Black is a shadow
Made by a person,
Black is a corner
With someone sitting there.

Black is when you close your eyes,
Black is deep and empty,
Black is a bad dream!

Andrew Taylor-Hall (12)
Archbishop Temple School

At The Races

At the races here today,
Oh what a beautiful day!
Engines roaring,
Engines breaking,
Then you hear the ambulance wailing at the races,
Here today, oh what a terrible day!

Curtis White (14)
Archbishop Temple School

Scottish Highlands

S tillness and tranquillity, the perfect peace
C alm winds stroke the branches of trees.
O sprey circle overhead curiously
T ow paths are sprinkled with a blanket of leaves.
T iny rodents scurry around in desperate search for food.
I nside I am filled with peace.
S himmering reflections from the lochs so still
H igh above my head pine trees lay a carpet of needles.

H azy mist as the sun sets in the distance
I cy fog throws a curtain over the landscape.
G hosts of gruelling battles faded, walk longingly into the darkness
H oping for eternal peace.
L andscapes bleached by the light of the moon
A ntlers of deer clash in a hardcore melée.
N atural happiness is how I describe this place.
D arkness is overcome with a warm glow
S unrise has come, another day in paradise begins.

Matthew Parkinson (12)
Archbishop Temple School

Around The World

I went around the world, you should have seen the things I saw,
I saw the Seven Wonders of the World,
I saw different people from different places,
I saw all kinds of creatures on land and in the sea,
I saw how different people dance and sing,
I saw what people eat, it's different from at home,
I saw that the world is not all that it seems to be,
Soooo . . .
I prayed for the hungry,
I prayed for the poor,
I prayed for the ill,
I prayed for the children without a home,
I prayed for the people all around the world.

Natalie Gibson (14)
Archbishop Temple School

My Film

In my film there is a great danger,
A battle of darkness and light,
The bustling of a darker metropolis
Hold the secrets of a race.

A bunch of misfits hold the key
To answer every mystery.

First there's Drake, hero bold and brave,
Then there's Rick, Mechanical Man,
JJ a mystical image,
Every film needs a beauty,
Well guess what, we have three,
Cat, Jess and Sara,
One cool, one fair, one sweet.
But alas we had a hero who went wrong,
He is Zane the venomous villain,
Who will stop our heroes one by one by one.

These heroes, will they win the battle?
These heroes, can they win the war?

They are ready,
The question is are you?

David Riley (12)
Archbishop Temple School

Shopping

Shopping trip coming up, can't wait,
Lots to buy, planning it with friends,
Then the bombshell - Mum's coming too!

Where will it be Preston, Blackpool, Manchester? No!
Special trip to Trafford Centre,
Great run for the bus, dash for the train,
Then hurry for the shuttle,
We're there at last.

Time for lunch, then shopping for real,
In and out like a butterfly,
Come on Mum, keep up,
Up the stairs,
Look over there, Claire's, Next, Tammy, Gap,
Tops to try, trousers, next the shoes,
Don't stop Mum.

Got your cards ready, need this top,
Oh! Is that the time,
There's still lots to do.

Dad's there waiting, groans at the bags,
Mum pulls a face,
'How much have you spent?'
'Don't ask, just drive,'
Next time go with your friends!

Yvonne Riley (14)
Archbishop Temple School

Sky

Sky is the clouds that fly above us,
Sky is the heavens that no one can see,
Sky is the space that never ends,
Sky is the place where the birds play,
The sky goes on forever and ever.

The sky is there every day,
Sky is blue or grey,
Sky is hot and cold,
Sky is where the sun lives,
Sky is the atmosphere,
Sky is no place for the devil,
At night you see twinkling stars in the sky.

Sky is the night and day,
The sky can be dark and sad
And can cry tears of rain,
Bats can fly in the night sky,
Lightning can flash and thunder can crash
And make bits of noisy sounds.

Christopher Clark (12)
Archbishop Temple School

Bus Stop

Boom, bang, pop, pow,
Oh man what am I gonna do now?
I think my engine's about to explode,
I need to pull over to the side of the road.
The car is smoking, I'm losing my vision,
I hope I don't get into a traffic collision.
I pray to Jesus, I cry Jehovah,
I think to myself, *oh my goodness!*
That sounds like my engine's busted.
Man I'm so stuck I've got no luck,
I've got to walk 10 miles just to call a tow truck.
It's been 3 hours and the punk can't find me,
The motorway patrol's pulling up behind me.
'Is this your car?'
'Yes, sir.'
'Well prove it.
By, the way you've got 4 hours to move it,
If it's still here when I come back around,
Your car's heading downtown to the impound.'
My car got towed by prejudiced cop,
I know tomorrow morning I'll be at the bus stop.

Adam Clarke (13)
Archbishop Temple School

Christmas Is Coming

Christmas is coming,
Hang up your stocking,
Christmas is coming on its way.
Christmas, Christmas, it's a happy day,
Full of children having fun,
Now that winter has come.

The elves are making all the toys,
For all the good little girls and boys.
Christmas is coming,
It's on its way!
Be good and Santa will visit you,
Be bad and you'll have no games to do.

Christmas is coming,
The nights are drawing in,
The lights are turning on
And the fun has just begun.

Rebecca Grant (13)
Archbishop Temple School

Spring

Springtime is my favourite season,
Maybe you can guess the reason.
Lambs bounce just like Tigger,
I hope no one will pull the trigger!

People with picnics in the park
And dogs running with an excited bark.
Boys all around playing football,
While small children are on the climbing wall.

Flowers come with a blush,
But the trees don't seem to rush.
An adventure has just begun,
So I hope you all can come.
There is so much to do
And I want to do it all with you!

Ashleigh Nickson (12)
Archbishop Temple School

Four Seasons

First comes spring, summer's coming,
Bees are ready to do their buzzing,
Trees and plants are growing fast,
Now that winter's in the past.

Summer's here, hot and nice,
Lying in the sun with a Coke and ice,
Having fun, playing on the street,
The heat of the pavements like ovens on your feet.

Next is autumn, goodbye heat!
Everyone's wearing wellies on their feet.
Leaves are falling all around,
Reds, yellows and oranges make a colourful playground.

Here is winter, Christmas is coming,
A white desert so cold, the chill is stunning!
My mind is blank, for wherever I go,
There will always be eternal snow.

Thomas Wiggins (12)
Archbishop Temple School

Santa, Please Don't Tell Me I've Been Bad

Merry Christmas are the words I like,
That's why I asked Santa if I could have a bike.

Decorations everywhere glowing so bright,
That's why I wish the stars were sparkling with light.

C hildren singing,
H aving a fab time.
R eindeers banging on my roof,
 I cicles are hanging from my front door.
S itting in my bed wishing what is next.
T ime to get up,
M ake my bed.
A ctually wake up my mum and dad,
S anta, please don't tell me I've been bad.

Daisy Short (14)
Archbishop Temple School

The Battle Of Hastings In 1066

1066 with King William we came
1066 we came from Normandy
1066 to get the land we wanted to claim
1066 this was not to be friendly
1066 we arrived in England
1066 I drew my sword
1066 to kill the men from Finland
1066 there was blood and gore
1066 we won the battle
1066 we won the fight
1066 with the noise of the metal
1066 we showed our might
1066 it was to London we rode
1066 we were to claim our new nation
1066 this was to be our new abode
1066 we witnessed the coronation
1066 so after setting out from France
1066 the army who thundered
1066 ended up with a great big dance
Because we killed the men who blundered.

Jonathan Chastney (12)
Archbishop Temple School

Autumn

Autumn leaves on the ground,
Autumn feeling all around.
The leaves are crunching when you walk,
You can see your breath when you talk.
The day is dark when you waken,
When you get home, the day's been taken.
Red and brown leaves on the trees,
People picking conkers upon their knees.
Autumn is windy so you can fly a kite,
When you go out you zip your coat up tight.

Lauren Townson (11)
Archbishop Temple School

Christmas Eve

Only three more hours to go,
But gosh won't those hours go slow.
I'm now lying in my bed,
Thoughts of presents rushing through my head.
As I try to get off to sleep,
I can't, so I try counting sheep.
When I finally shut my eyes,
I dream of scrumptious Christmas pies.
As the grandfather clock strikes four,
I get excited more and more.
I do hope I receive a bike,
For that is something I really would like.
I wonder if it's snowing outside
And then on the ice, I can slide.
I really can't wait for morning to come
And then I can wake up my dad and mum.
Thankfully morning has finally arrived,
I can open my presents with pride.

Amy Burgess (12)
Archbishop Temple School

Love

Love is a crazy thing, it drives you up the wall
So when you meet that perfect boy, make sure he isn't small
I don't believe in Cupid, you have to make your own luck
I know it sounds crazy, but just do it by the book.

Love is a gentle thing, handle it with care
You'll be mental to do it as a dare
To be in love you need to think, *he's mine, he's mine, he's mine*
You'll start thinking about the future, those quiet nights in with wine.

Your whole world will revolve around him
You'll forget your mates, Hannah and Jim
But don't be stupid, your friends mean more
Because when he dumps you, your friends will be there for sure.

Briony Wilks (12)
Archbishop Temple School

Holidays

I love a holiday,
We go somewhere different every year.
Preston's OK,
But sometimes we go far away, sometimes near.

Once we went to York,
We went to a restaurant there,
First I had some pork,
Finished off with a nice juicy pear.

Another time we went to France,
We went there by a ferry.
I learned this great new dance,
I did look rather merry!

The worst holiday was Venice,
Because I fell in the water!
My dad must have been embarrassed
As he pretended I wasn't his daughter!

My favourite holiday was Spain,
It was ever so sunny,
It never decided to rain
But Costa del Sol costa lot of de money!

You can go back by plane,
By ferry or by boat,
By bus or by train,
But a helicopter gets my vote!

Back home now
It was fun, as I said
Adios, au revoirs and ciâo!
It's good to be back in my own bed.

Elizabeth Brookes (12)
Archbishop Temple School

He Left Me

I thought we were going to be together, just him and me,
I dreamt about it every night, my forthcoming fantasy,
But one day on the way to school, he took the wrong bend,
When those huge heinous tyres brought it to an end.

No one at school knew who did it or why,
And no one ever knew today he would die.
I could hear the echo of his voice still fresh in my mind
And I cry thinking the rustle of the leaves call out his name . . .

His eyes were deep liquid pools of chocolate,
I never thought he'd be in pools of blood,
His head was a mass of golden grains of sand,
I never thought it would lie where he stood.

Over and over in my mind
I hear the sound of the tyres grind,
And often wonder if he'd gone the right way,
Would he still be alive today?

The world seems pointless to live in now,
My dreams are rivers of blackness,
He died so young, it seems so pointless
That I am alive when he's not . . .

I think to myself such terrible things,
I will murder the man who murdered him,
I will use every knife and gun I have,
Until he screams his last thread of living.

I will pray for him like the Pope,
Soon I will join him.
I guess it was his destiny
He left me . . .

Sita Bridglal (14)
Archbishop Temple School

Motorbikes

Engines roaring, forks bouncing,
The flags flying, the crowds shouting,
The pistons pumping,
All in a day's work for a motorbike racer.

Triumph, Suzuki, Yamaha,
All these names rivalling Hyabusa,
All in order the bikes line up waiting for the light to turn green,
All in a day's work for a motorbike racer.

The light turns green, they shoot off like speeding bullets.
The speed is high, reaching 150, they brake suddenly
When they come into the hairpin,
All in a day's work for a motorbike racer.

After the race the choppers come out, fabrication
And graphics and many more,
Pumped up tyres, new carburettors and gears,
All in day's work for a motorbike racer.

Sam Biddle (14)
Archbishop Temple School

Food

Ice cream is so cold and smooth, waiting on your spoon,
But when you put it in your mouth, your body will go cool.
Ice cream is the coldest thing that you will ever taste,
So if you don't like getting cold, stick to chicken paste!

Chips are so warm and tasty when you get them from the pan,
That you gobble down your portion as quickly as you can.
So if you come to mine for tea when we are having chips,
Cover them with ketchup and you will lick your lips!

Crisps are so light and crunchy as you eat them from your hand,
I always have Walkers, as they're my favourite brand.
If you only eat one bag a day, your body will stay healthy
And sometimes in special packs, they can make you very wealthy!

Sarah Latham (11)
Archbishop Temple School

Senses

A world without sight
They say 'out of sight, out of mind' how mistaken they were
How do you imagine a sunset?
A spectacular and inspirational formation of colour. You can't.
A smile, the look in someone's eyes, expressions, they portray
                                                    so much.
A world without sight is a blank canvas, no colours, no smiles, nothing.

A world without sound.
A baby's chatter, their first words
A mother without that, but knowing it's there. Torture.
Background noise is everywhere, annoying, but somehow necessary
An applause, laughter, music. It's everywhere.
A world without sound is isolation
As if watching the world and your life pass you by
From within a silent prison.

A world without touch.
No hugs, no texture, no sensation. Nothing.
Water running through your fingers, a baby's head, warm and downy.
Comfort has no meaning, no value.

A world without taste.
Without the mouth-watering goodness of fresh fruit.
No sweetness, bitterness, blandness, sourness.
Nothing to separate the food you eat
Just food, no enjoyment about it.

A world without smell.
No coffee, flowers, freshness, the mouth-watering smells of cooking.
None of it. Nothing.

A world without sense is blank, utterly bare, a barren wilderness,
                                                    a desert.

No sensation, nothing.

Rebecca Senior (15)
Archbishop Temple School

Friendship

Friends are stars in the sky,
They make the meaning of life go up so high!
Friends are there for you all the time,
It doesn't matter whether we're at her house or mine!

Friends are people who won't regret,
They like to forgive and forget,
China, France, the British Isles,
They'll keep in touch no matter how many miles.

Friends are trustworthy and funny,
They go out whether it's rainy or sunny.
Friends will respect your opinions in each and every way,
They will care for you day after day.

My friends are like four leaf clovers . . .
Rare to find, but lucky to have.

Emilie Hulme (12)
Archbishop Temple School

Christmas

The songs are being sung,
The stockings are being hung
And the children go off to play.
Here we are waiting
For the family to come and stay.
I hope I have a brilliant day.

C hildren singing carols,
H ere are lots more,
R unning through the snow,
 I cicles all around,
S anta's sleigh is coming down,
T urkey dinner is being made,
M ore, more, more,
A s the day has come to a draw
S now falls more.

Rachael Williams (14)
Archbishop Temple School

Friendship

What is friendship?
Is it a special bond between people?
Is friendship like a warm summer's day,
When the sun smiles down at the children who play?

What is friendship?
Is it a special bond between people?
Is friendship like the cold, wet rain,
When each tiny drop is filled with pain?

What is friendship?
Is it a special bond between people?
Friendship is like the deep sea waves,
When friends argue, they don't talk for days,
But when the raging storm calms down
Friends make up again, so they won't drown.

Friendship is like a circle,
It has no end,
You never really know who a friend is
Until you lose one.
It's only when they have gone
You will know
How much a friend means to you.

Treat all your friends with respect,
As everyone should know,
A friend is a friend
Even when they have gone.
Just remember,
Friendship is a bond between you and someone.

Neela Dookhun (14)
Archbishop Temple School

Bonfire Night

Showers of sparkles falling down,
Silently, silently, without a sound.
Waiting in suspense we hold on tight,
Just waiting for the dazzles to fill the night.
This one shines with splendour bright,
Then falls and fades out of our sight.
This star's gone, gone in a flash,
But we're waiting for the next one to crash.
The one is a rocket, it glints and gleams,
Flying through the sky, what a colourful scene.
We've come to the end of the flashes and flickers,
But still the pretty November stars twinkle.
Now we move our eyes back down to the ground,
Where whirling amber flames are found.
Gathered round the fire keeping warm,
Surrounded with November peace and calm.
We listen a while, watching the blaze,
The dancing flames cause us to sink into a daze.
As we remember winters past,
We hope this silken serenity lasts.
Underneath the twilight sky,
We watch the dancing flames slowly die,
We watch the dancing flames slowly die . . .

Naomi Atkinson (14)
Archbishop Temple School

I Cannot Wait . . .

Rain, rain, rain, driving me insane,
I watch as it drips down the windowpane.
Soon I will look out and the sun will shine bright,
Fun, laughter and exciting thoughts.

My holiday will be so great,
Only two days, I cannot wait.
My suitcase is packed, I'm ready to go,
All I need now is the taxi to show.

I cannot wait to bathe by the pool,
Laughing and joking as the boys play cool.
I cannot wait to swim in the sea,
Along with the fishes in there with me.

I cannot wait to lay on the sand,
Feeling both good and grand.
I cannot wait to taste the different food,
That will put me in the party mood.

I hope the sun will shine like a star,
Bright, bold, standing out from afar.
I cannot wait to see the amazing sights
Although I am frightened of the great heights.

My time on holiday will soon fly by,
Left with memories that will bring a tear to my eye.

Chloe Anderton (14)
Archbishop Temple School

On Her Wedding Day

Arrived at the church at quarter-past two,
With the grass still glistening from the morning dew.
The guests pile in like an army of ants,
Grandad's already drunk, we're having to listen to him rant.
Will she turn up, we pray,
On her wedding day?

Small children running, dressed in their best,
Nothing's too fine for the wedding guests.
Everyone's wearing their brand new clothes,
Strutting around with an elegant pose.
What will the bride say
On her wedding day?

The congregation waits with anticipation,
To marvel at the bride's wonderful creation.
The bride arrives and waits a while,
She glances round with a nervous smile.
She wipes her tears away,
On her wedding day.

'I do,' said the bride. 'I do,' said the groom,
There wasn't a dry eye in the room.
The confetti fluttered like leaves from the trees,
Everybody laughed as the photographer cried, *'Cheese!'*
Her worries went away,
On her wedding day.

Hannah Almond (14)
Archbishop Temple School

The Teacher

They file in, as quickly as their small legs could,
They knew they shouldn't be late,
They knew they couldn't be late,
They knew they mustn't be late
For the teacher.

He slammed the door shut behind them,
He knew he should scare them,
He knew his staring eyes could scare them,
He knew who his tiny target must be today,
Did the teacher.

'Johnson!' he began, a sick smile grew on his ghastly face,
Johnson knew he should his eyes now,
Johnson knew he couldn't panic now,
Johnson knew he mustn't be scared now,
Of the teacher.

He demanded an answer to the question asked,
He knew he should make it hard,
He knew he could make it difficult,
He knew he must make it torture,
Did the teacher.

Johnson walked slowly up to the terrifying table,
Johnson knew he should run away,
Johnson knew he could run away,
From the teacher.

Amy McDowell (14)
Archbishop Temple School

The Dawn Patrol

As dawn breaks
Figures can be seen,
Figures carrying strange-shaped objects,
These figures all seem to be headed the same way,

Towards the place where land meets water
And the water curves upwards,
Reaching for the sky.
The tip of the water turns white
And crashes back down.

The figures reach the golden stretch,
But continue towards the water,
These figures begin to walk through the water,
They throw their objects down.

These objects float,
The first figure gets out of his depth,
He jumps astride his object and lies down,
He starts to use his arms
To propel himself further out.

He sees the water rise up
And quickly turns his object round,
The water carries him forward,
All of a sudden he rises
And stands on the object.

The water carries him forward and he weaves back and forth,
Perfectly balanced on his object,
The object is a surfboard,
The figures are surfers,
They are the dawn patrol.

Tom Kirby (15)
Archbishop Temple School

Sensing Christmas

Faces of people
Holding their christingles up to God,
Excitement rises as Christmas Day approaches,
Flames of the candles dancing in the draught,
Empty manger in the nativity scene,
Sounds of carols echoing in the church longing for the baby,
Sounds of angels singing glory to God,
A baby crying but she belongs to us,
Silence then the flicking of the page.

'Once in Royal David's city . . .'
Orangey scent lingers with the christingles,
Smell of burning candles,
Warm smell of people huddled together,
Musty aroma of wet bodies heating up,
Incense of smoke as the candles are extinguished,
Rubbery skin of the orange,
Spiky cocktail sticks,
Red ribbon of blood.

A gift passes between hands,
A hug of Christmas cheer,
Sweets of the christingle,
Raisins one by one,
At midnight bread and wine,
Jesus' body and blood,
Clock chimes twelve.

Christmas comes,
New day,
Peace at last.

Anna Gelasia Sheasby (14)
Archbishop Temple School

My Death

I pace around the living room, waiting for him to arrive.
I hear a sudden bang of the door, then he slowly creeps up the drive.
I start to shiver when I hear his deep breaths getting nearer
And nearer to my door.
I know why he is here because I have disobeyed his law.
I jump vigorously as he mows down my fragile front door.
I beg for my life and say, 'You loved me once before.'
I see him charge for me and feel the hard slap across my face.
I fall to the floor at a tremendous, fast pace.
He digs me once, he digs me twice as I feel my legs break.
I cry out for mercy and think how much more can I take?
I hear him shout, I hear me scream, I see in his eyes he has no fear.
I see him slowly draw the knife from his pouch,
The blade getting very near.
Then all of a sudden the knife goes in and I hear,
'Hello I'm Death, and I am here!'

Yasmin Mogra (14)
Archbishop Temple School

Birds

Up in the trees dancing with the leaves, birds prance with joy!
They fly through the air like a jumping, elegant hare
and sway from side to side.
Some fly low, picking worms as they go
whilst others fly high making their prey cry!
Birds sing their own tune even in the gloom with each one not alike.
They bring peace to the Earth and were created at its birth,
isn't it amazing!
Do you like birds?
I like them too because if I cry they lift me high and I feel happy at last.
Birds are great, they stay with their mate
and love to swim and fish.
Birds are pretty, but isn't it a pity that they get hunted every day?
Birds are free, so let them be.

Oliver Malcolm-Gregson (11)
Archbishop Temple School

Black Beauty

To see is to live, all the beauty in the world right before my eyes,
I know it's there, but it's no longer clear,
The world's a blur, does the beauty stop here?
Nothing but blackness and memories of beauty.

'As blind as a bat!' I hear them murmur,
I can't see their faces,
They don't see me in many cases.
Nothing but blackness, pushing the beauty away.

A painful thud, as I crash into the door frame,
I ask, 'Who put that there?'
I'm talking to myself and feel deep despair.
Nothing but blackness and pain as beauty dies.

The tears roll down my invisible face,
I don't see where they land,
Does it matter? Life's quite bland.
Nothing but blackness, and me with my thoughts,
My thoughts . . .

To see is to live, or that's what they say,
Maybe they're right, but beauty can be found,
I can feel the breeze and hear the sounds.
So much more than blackness, the beauty is so clear.

Life is for living, whatever hand you're dealt,
It may not be fair,
But I shouldn't care.
Nothing but blackness and the joy that life brings.

'She's blind but brave,' I hear them say,
I can't see their faces,
But I know they see me, in many cases.
Nothing but blackness and the beauty of life.

Keira Gilchrist (14)
Archbishop Temple School

The Curtain Has Now Fallen . . .

The curtain has now fallen
For the play to continue.
My fall is for you
And my love is within you.
The first time you cut me
I knew the blood would never stop
And my razor sharp claws
Another unavailing prop.
You know me stripped,
Gloves off and hands tied,
You know from what I run
And know the secrets I hide.
In the ashen reflection,
Of the moon tonight,
I'm pitiful, anonymous,
There's no need to fight.
Pull away my mask
And my costume of fear,
Wrap your hands round my neck
And I won't shed a tear.
My bravery is spent
On my actions untold,
My heart is in your hand,
In your hand so cold.

Charlotte McKee (14)
Archbishop Temple School

The Dream World

Close your eyes, drift off to sleep,
Off to dream world,
Mystical, amazing deep sleep.

Do you want to be a hero
And soar above the clouds,
Or dive deep below zero?

Or you could be the greatest of them all,
A complete daredevil,
Ready to take any jump, any fall.

Maybe you just want to stay calm,
Have someone to protect you,
Keep you safe from harm.

Whatever world you choose, don't hurry,
You have eight hours to dream,
Don't rush, don't hurry.

Your dream is a blank screen,
You just have to paint it,
Then go dream, dream . . .

Just remember though,
Dreams can be as calm as a summer morning,
Or wild like a cheetah,
So sleep, dream, fly away, *go!*

Helen-Ema Calvert (12)
Archbishop Temple School

November

Bonfire Night,
The sky is alight
With fireworks bright
In the cold, dark night.

Boom! Bang! Buzz! Bash!
Sparklers spin and rockets crash!
Children scream with pure delight
At flying sparks in the cold, dark night.

Catherine wheels twiz and twirl
As Roman candles whizz and whirl.
Fireworks climb to a spectacular height
Through the black cloak of the cold, dark night.

But Bonfire Night is a time to remember,
'Remember, remember the fifth of November'.
Crime, punishment, torture, death,
Deadly plots and a dying breath.

In six days' time we'll remember the war,
The terrible sights that the soldiers saw,
Killing, dying, forced to fight,
Trying to survive in the cold, dark night.

To try to stop it happening again
Don't forget and it won't be in vain,
In the cold, dark month of November,
Please take time to remember.

Lizzie Parsons (14)
Archbishop Temple School

Animals

Animals are living creatures, who bring us no harm,
Some are cute and cuddly, while others live in the sea.
Others have scales and great big teeth, but bring no alarm,
Most are big and like to fight, yet some are smaller than me.

Fish are small and multicoloured,
Lions are big and scary,
Rhinos huge! But never bothered
And monkeys cute, petite and hairy.

Monkeys like to make a sound,
Screeching, jumping all around,
Elephants, quiet as a mouse,
Standing still like a house.

Giraffes stand with their necks all tall,
Birds fly freely through the sky,
Yet from the air they never fall,
With tiny mice, climbing high.

Squirrels up high, in the trees,
Playing happily with the bees,
Birds flying overhead,
Colours, like blue and red.

Dogs and cats both make great pets,
Cuddly and so fun,
Not to be cooped up in nets,
We love animals like day loves sun!

Abigail Green (12)
Archbishop Temple School

Friendship

Friends are like strawberries with cream,
Friends are there when you are in crisis,
They are always helpful and kind.
Friends can comfort you,
Without friends you would be lost,
A friend is like a mug with a saucer.

If you don't have friends, you are lonely and sad,
When you are with friends you have fun, fun!
What can you do without friends?
Nothing!
If you don't have friends, you are lonely and sad.

You will be like toast without butter if you don't have them,
When you go on days out you scream and have fun,
If you fall out with one, go to another.
Friends can share all of your secrets,
If you have got friends, you will shine like the sun,
Friends are like sugar, spice and all things nice.

Naomi Saint (12)
Archbishop Temple School

Tomorrow

The future holds adventure, an unknown way of life,
Possibly a world of hope, or endless trouble and strife.
The grass may no longer be green, the sky no longer blue,
We can only be certain of what we know is true.

The seasons may have vanished, resulting in endless rain
Or the sun's rays may flow continuously like an ongoing train.
Stars which once shone brightly, now are dull and grey,
They are buttons which have been rubbed and worn away.

Trees as tall as tower blocks will have sprung up over the years,
Or will these trees be extinct, confirming our current fears?
Paper and pencils may be a thing of the past,
Everyone with computers and laptops, doing things twice as fast.

The world will keep on turning, twenty-four hours a day,
Resulting in new days in which to work, rest and play.
Tomorrow is a new day, where nothing is the same,
People may find hope, faith, love, courage or fame.

Janet Barton (14)
Archbishop Temple School

New Year's Eve!

Singing, dancing, having fun,
A new year's nearly begun.
The party is now in full swing,
No one can eat another thing.

Ten minutes to go,
Resolutions start to flow,
The music's playing loud and clear
Like an explosion in our ears.

Now there's only one minute to go,
The bubbly's poured, we're raring to go,
Out come the party poppers,
Pop, bang, fizz!
The fireworks and sparklers start to whizz.
Auld Lang Syne we start to sing,
Big Ben's chimes start to ring,
The countdown starts from ten to one,
Say goodbye to last year it's nearly gone.

Let's look forward with hope and cheer,
To welcome in a brand new year.

Lucy Crook (14)
Archbishop Temple School

I Don't Want To Go To School Today

I don't want to go to school today,
That little girl in my class had another bruise.
I don't want to go to school today,
She'll never beat them, she'll always lose.
I don't want to go to school today,
They always kick her down in the corridors.
I don't want to go to school today,
Everyone just walks by and ignores.
I don't want to go to school today,
All the girls poke fun of her in PE.
I don't want to go to school today,
She's now in the newspapers, all over TV.
I don't want to go to school today,
Everyone keeps crying, staring at where she used to sit.
I don't want to go to school today,
To remember all the sad times she was brutally hit.
I don't want to go to school today,
Now everyone remembers the lonely little girl, now they see.
I don't want to go to school today,
Because that little girl was me.

Amber Watson (14)
Archbishop Temple School

AD 3000

Trees, burnt
Water, poisoned
Air, black
Yet we still go on.

Days, dismal
Nights, torture
Life, dwindling
Yet the war is almost won.

Food, scarce
Enemies, close
Defeat, near
Yet battle still commences.

Hopes, gone
Morale, destroyed
Retreat, available
Yet we build up our defences.

Death, upon us
Life, leaving us
Will, left us
Yet we don't give in to their demand.

War, constant
Peace, impossible
Fear, everywhere
This is life in AD 3000.

Elliott Park (14)
Archbishop Temple School

Hallowe'en!

It's a damn cold night,
It's hard to spot any light,
Children out giving frights,
While trick or treating with delight!

A pumpkin's face in the window,
A skeleton at your door,
A scary mask, a witch's cat,
With lots of blood and gore!

A Frankenstein, a vampire,
A witch and Dracula too,
A witch's broom, a cauldron
Vein, blood and eyeball stew!

A full moon sailing through the air,
A werewolf on a hill
Oh, oh, oh please help me,
Please I'm on my bill.

The night is coming to an end now,
I'm on my long trek home,
But will I find my way now?
How I wish I had my phone!

I'm at the haunted mansion,
The creaking of the door! *Eeeek!*
An angry voice shouted out . . .
'Welcome to Grim Galore!
Ha, ha, ha!'

Chris Glover (12)
Archbishop Temple School

There I Live On 28

There I live on 28,
With my family, there I wait.
In the garden is a pond,
Where all my fish swim and bond.
Up above is a lonely tree,
Standing there with no one to see.
He lets go, all his leaves,
As they dance to take a breath.
The grass joins in as the party starts,
But the best of course is its dark brown bark.
Round the corner is a long black drive,
She gobbles up cars that come and drive.
The pond's best friend is the waterfall,
As the water escapes the spiders crawl.
But best of all is our big house,
It's too posh for a sneaky little mouse.
First of all it targets its prey,
Chews then spits for it to run away.
Our fence is a shield as black as ink,
If you're lucky enough it may give you a wink.
So that's my house on 28.

Victor Chow (12)
Archbishop Temple School

Fireworks

'Remember, remember the 5th of November,
Gunpowder, treason and plot'.
A night of fun and laughter for all,
For others possibly not.
With the strike of a match
Or the burst of a flame,
The night could go wrong and end up in pain,
Although they are beautiful
And light up the sky,
Fireworks turn on you quickly
In the blink of an eye.
Childish games that always seem fun
Or drunken fools that won't see the sun.
The pain they can cause,
The damage they do,
If only they'd think,
If only they knew.
Fireworks are fun
And we'll never fear,
But bad things can happen
When you play with fire . . .

Vicki Holden (14)
Archbishop Temple School

Dad's Going Away Again!

Off he goes again,
Marching into war, like a proud peacock, stood tall like a cliff
With Americans at his side, as his 'allies'.

He has left many times before,
But that doesn't make me miss him less.
It's like a piece of me gets lost but always come back.

Last time he wrote me a letter,
Describing the poor, plagued, persecuted people he gave aid to.
All they could say in English was Beckham'.

This time he will be gone for six months,
He'll miss Christmas and new year,
Mum's birthday, she now will not celebrate with cheer.

He will save people's lives,
He will treat illnesses that otherwise would have killed,
He will give families the chance to see a loved one again.

He is part of a plan to make a war-torn Iraq peaceful,
He can help them regain independence and stability,
He will make the people's lives better.

I miss him when he's gone,
Love him more each day,
But Dad please come home safe, I pray.

Danni Harrison (14)
Archbishop Temple School

My Rabbit Thumper

My rabbit Thumper is a cheeky little bun,
He can sometimes be naughty,
But he has a lot of fun.

He's cute, he's friendly, he's funny,
He's also inquisitive too,
He's a really happy bunny,
I hope you think so too.

But one day he was really naughty,
I thought he was gonna get punished
And then he saw my car,
He put his front paws on the roof and kicked with his back,
He escaped into the hall and was too scared to come back.

Thumper is white and grey,
His ears are grey and long,
He bounces non-stop all day.

Thumper's a clever bun,
I hope he doesn't run away,
He's cool, he's smart, he gets lots of food a day,
So I don't know why he would anyway.

It's a shame he's all alone all day,
With no one else to play,
But when we come home we wonder how lively can you be?

Sam Hughes (11)
Archbishop Temple School

Bullying

I'm standing here on my own,
Wishing I could be at home.
I look around the playground, children having fun,
But here I am on my own wondering what I've done.
I see them coming, I look away,
They start trouble, what do I say?

'Hey you, Billy No Mates,'
It's him that everyone hates, hates, hates.
A shiver runs down my spine,
Why is it me all the time?
The bell rings, it's time to go in,
Everyone's shoving me towards the bin.

I'm in the classroom at my desk,
I've got a question and I'm too scared to ask.
They're sat behind me kicking my chair,
Now I have chewing gum stuck in my hair.
We are waiting quietly for the teacher,
But on my back I then feel a creature.

The bell rings, it's time to go home at last,
Out of school I run very fast.
The bus is here, it's about to go,
Soon I think I'll be on the floor.
I catch the bus, I'm on my way home,
So soon I won't be on my own.

Joanne Cottam (14)
Archbishop Temple School

Conway Park

As I approach the pitch at ten to ten,
All I see is grass and trees.
As more people arrive,
I know it's nearly time for the *match!*

When I'm in the changing room getting dressed,
I start to feel excited like never before.
As I run out onto the pitch,
I see the birds in the tops of the trees
And look at the area surrounding me.
All I see is concrete and houses,
The mud is spread over the pitch like butter and bread.
When you stand on the grass it springs back up
Like an indestructible robot.
When the whistle blows it pierces the ears of the spectators,
Like an ear-splitting gun.

My hair is blown back in the wind
And the manager's coat nearly flies off him.
What is going to happen . . . ?
As the atmosphere increases step by step
You feel on top of the world,
But suddenly . . . it's all over.
We survived this week but what will await us another time?
The crisp packets blow around the pitch
And the park rests until next time.

Luke Jenner (13)
Archbishop Temple School

My Best Friend

My best friend can't count, 1, 2, 3,
My best friend can't say, a, b, c,
But my best friend is clever you see
Because my best friend is special to me!

My best friend comes out to play
And comes with me on my holiday,
Is much more fun than I can say
And special to me in his own way.

My best friend is as cuddly as can be
With only a care to be with me,
Over the ocean into the sea
That's where he and I will be.

My best friend, well have you guessed,
No? Yeah?
Because my best friend . . .
Is my big brown bear!

Hannah Wright (12)
Archbishop Temple School

Winter

Winter is cold,
Winter is white,
Winter makes it snow,
Winter makes me wear a coat,
   Winter.

The sun doesn't shine,
In winter it is not warm.
We don't go to school in winter,
In winter it becomes Christmas.
Winter is magical.
   Winter.

Winter is fun,
In the snow you can run,
You can slide on the ice,
You can make a snowman.

I love winter,
I like winter,
Oh winter.

Daniel McCormick (14)
Archbishop Temple School

The Funny Birds

The funny birds live in the forest,
They all come to their calling mistress.
They're the funniest birds from all around,
Too bad that most of them drowned!

They all wear a horrible fluffy mane!
But never will they ever gain,
A single little golden penny,
Because they can't do jobs . . . it's too much of a strain.

But great warriors they are,
But can't resist having a drink at a bar!
Never will they ever fly,
No flap, flap . . . just a cry.

They have homes called Martons,
The big homes are made from Ribena cartons!
They need big houses for their huge tummies,
Because they can't stop eating teddy bear gummies!

They were like a very long rainbow,
The reds run the forest like fire,
The pinks are like blooming flowers
And the yellows, of course, are the golden heart of it all.

Elizabeth Johnston (12)
Archbishop Temple School

Dragons

Dragons are mighty, dragons roar
They hardly ever touch the floor.
Dragons eat rabbits,
Dragons eat snakes,
A dragon eats anything it takes.
Dragons are red, dragons are gold,
Some are even covered in mould!
Dragons are bronze, dragons are blue
(And if you lived in the Arctic, you would be too.)
Dragons are black
Some so scary, you'll have a heart attack.
Just to show you how bad dragon breath is,
Here is a story from the ancient land of Keniz.
There once was a dragon called Kashan,
And a warrior from Smashan.
The warrior pulled a sword . . .
And the dragon's breath sent him to the hospital ward.
I can still smell that breath now,
Well how would you survive it, how?
Don't kiss the dragons
Or you will only have just enough life to say, 'Wow!'

Jordan Thompson (11)
Archbishop Temple School

Cats

Out they go, prowl, prowl,
They are like a ball of cotton.
Wonder what they do, prowl, prowl.
Out at night, all alone in the dark.
We think they are cute and cuddly,
They might think otherwise, prowl, prowl.

Hiss! Miaow!
'Shut up,' say the neighbours!
Singing or fighting, they find something to do,
They are as cute as can be,
Do they like cat food and biscuits?
Who knows? Only they do.
Wonder what they dream about,
Food and cotton balls maybe.

Crash!
There goes the kitchen plate!
Bang!
There goes the broom!
They are mischievous and naughty,
Cute and cuddly . . .
Or are they?

Watch out for them,
They could be lurking anywhere,
They sing like an opera singer (not),
If you don't treat them right,
Then they could come and . . .
Get you . . . !
Prowl, prowl, prowl . . .

Abbi Hough (12)
Archbishop Temple School

Birthdays

Birthdays are great days!
We giggle and gobble on our faces,
We play on our races.
We're crashing and bashing,
Laughing and screaming.
We love our birthdays!

Birthdays are cheerful times!
Joyful and graceful chimes . . .
We dance in our dresses,
We sing with our voices,
She dances like a butterfly,
She sings like a bird,
We love our birthdays.

Birthdays are periods of expectations!
We wish on our full imaginations . . .
The time of our birthday wishes,
Wishing for a present in our birthday bashes,
We are angels,
Flying high in our sky,
We love our birthdays!

Birthdays are loving days!
We hug and kiss and we play . . .
Birthdays are surreal times,
We look at our faces at charming times.
We love the type of presents we get,
The day we will never forget.
Our birthdays,
Great days!

Grace Xia (12)
Archbishop Temple School

Horses

Horses are graceful,
Horses are fast,
Horses have power within their grasp.

Horses are high spirited,
Horses love grass,
Horses are great, they never come last.

Horses should never be bad or sad,
Horses are never glum,
Horses just want to have fun!

Horses run
And horses jump,
Over the moonlit sky.

Horses race to win,
Horses race for fun,
Horses win prizes for everyone.

Horses are ace,
Horses are beautiful,
Horses should never be mistreated.

Horses will never die,
They'll always be my favourite,
So goodbye . . .

Rowena Astin (12)
Archbishop Temple School

My Match Today

I am going to a match today
So I can see my favourite team play
I am going to cheer them on
Whilst I bang the big drum.

When we score
I jump up and roar
Then sit back down
And look around
To see everyone smiling.

At half-time I get a drink
And then I begin to think
If they hadn't scored
I would be very bored
And I would have wanted to go.

But instead I am here
Without any fear
Of losing the game
Or their fame.

At the end
I am shouting, 'Defend,'
So we would win our match
At last we have won
It's over and done.

Sam McGrievy-Smith (12)
Archbishop Temple School

Sunday

Ding-dong, ding-dong,
the church bells start to ring.
Dashing through the village, pulling up my socks,
collection in my pocket, tying back my locks.
Hymn book, frill, collection, Psalter -
carrying the cross I must not falter.
Singing, sermon, prayers and chants,
are so much better than my mother's rants!
It leaves me feeling warm inside,
before I dash off, my horse to ride . . .

He's always waiting by the gate,
I can honestly say he's my best mate.
He throws his head and pricks his ears,
my heart's so full, I brim with tears.
I groom, I stroke, I tell my tales,
I know he's there when all else fails.
I tack him up and off we go,
through the village, very slow.
Past the church and through the gate,
Galloping together - God, me, and my very best mate.

Beth Horsley (12)
Archbishop Temple School

When I Was Famous!

When I was famous I was in love with a man,
He went by the name of Tom Tank.
He would stand there and say, 'Hip, hip, hooray.'
At the end of one of my plays.
He wore grey shoes covered in booze
And a top hat made of white silk.
A grey suit with a splodge here and there
And a tie made out of wool.
Oh why, oh why did I let him go?

When I was famous I went to an awards ceremony,
I stepped out of my limo in a sparkling gold dress
And matching gold shoes.
I walked to the red carpet, there it lay excited and staring up at me,
I stepped on it like a cautious crocodile.
The fans started calling my name
I was as nervous as can be,
I walked down the red carpet with pride in my soul.
I gave a twirl at the end and waved goodbye to my fans.

I had a great time when I was famous!

Charlotte Feeny (11)
Archbishop Temple School

The Beautiful Game

The crowd *roar* as the players come on!
The ref gets ready to blow, game on!
I eat my food, ready to go,
The opposition scores, 'Oh no!'

A player on my team gets sent off the field,
The club mascot boos, I know how he feels.
The crowd rise to their feet, they stamp and applaud.
My little sister next to me simply looks bored.

We try our best to score after half-time,
Our forward zigzags along the touchline,
But is knocked off his feet by a wall-like defender,
All of 6ft 6" and unwilling to surrender.

The keeper gets the ball, kicks it high and scores!
The away fans moan and groan, they're heading for the doors.
Our fans are celebrating, they think it's all over and it is at last . . .
Until next week when we're here again, the time will go so fast.

David Robinson (12)
Archbishop Temple School

Cats!

Cats, oh I love cats
They're loads better than rats
They have stolen my heart
Right from the start!
I love their fur, so silky and smooth
And have you noticed they're always on the move?

In the mornings the curl up on your bed
It's as if they're trying to say, 'Wake up sleepyhead!'
I adore their cute, beady eyes
But I hate saying my goodbyes
When you start to shout, out they run
Away from argument 6,001!

If you buy a house-trained pet
Then you will never have a cleaning debt
I love their little, cute, mischievous ways
Because they can brighten up any of your dullest days
I hate anyone yelling at them at any time
Because they're not anyone else's, they're all mine!

Nicola Wilson (12)
Archbishop Temple School

In The Future

In the future, what will be of me?
Will I have the same personality?
Will I be so very blonde and fair
Or will I have a ghastly stare?
Will I have such gorgeous looks
Or will people say I belong with the ducks?
When I'm older will I get a job
Or might children name me the 'lazy slob'?
When I'm ancient will I go so grey
Or will some kids ask me out to play?
Will I ever have a dreamboat hunk?
Will that dreamboat then get sunk?
In the future will I have a child
Or will my soul become so wild?
Will my life be full of sorrow
Or will I be able to live for tomorrow?
In the future what will be of me
So in my future, surprise me!

Grace Conlon (11)
Archbishop Temple School

Football Is The Greatest Game Around

Football is the greatest game around
It's got passion, love and joy,
The players are amazing and so are the huge grounds
And so is the Sky sports analyser, Tim Lovejoy.

The roar of the crowd is breath-taking
The players' behaviour changes as they walk over the white line
The taste of defeat is heartbreaking
But the joy of winning is like a fine wine.

The football turf is sacred
The lush, green grass is as smooth as a new carpet
Which fills the poorer players with dread
The crowds band plays along to the rhythm of a solo trumpet.

When the final whistle blows there are mixed emotions
Players either down in the dumps or bubbling
The managers give their commiserations or congratulations
After a tiring ninety minutes, they all go into the bath tumbling.

Football is the greatest game around.

Andrew Johnson (12)
Archbishop Temple School

Friends

I'll never forget the times we cried,
The times we laughed, the times we lied.
The good, the bad,
And all the sad.

When we go places together,
We go whatever the weather.
We always go to town,
Wearing always a smile and never a frown.

When one of us is feeling blue,
We stick together, just like glue.
We always make each other happy,
Especially when we're being snappy.

We always make each other smile,
It stands out for a mile
We never fall out
That's what friendship's about.

We hang out at school
My best friend's so cool.
We talk to each other all the time,
She even helped me make this rhyme.

We give each other all our trust,
I hope it never goes bust.
She's nice and kind
And I could never find a better friend . . .
Than mine!

Nicola Doolan (13)
Archbishop Temple School

If I Was Famous . . .

If I was famous
Or a great big star
I'd always be seen
In my stretch limo car
When I'm walking in the city
I see all my fans
They'll all be trying to grab me
With their claw-like hands.

When I'm seen in public I'll never
Look a mess
Nearly everyone will see me
In my 2 million pound dress
All my fans are waiting
And everyone I pass
They'll stick their pen and paper at me
And say, 'Can I have your autograph?'

If you go to a theatre,
You'll see my name in lights
I'll be acting in that theatre
Many days and nights
And then I'll get *really* big
And start to have a massive gig
All those little kids out there
When they're older I know who they want to be
Every one of them
Will want to be . . . *me!*

Sarah Fisher (11)
Archbishop Temple School

Maybe When I'm Thirty

Maybe when I'm thirty,
I'll have a great big house
I might be married to a guy called Drake
I might have a cute pet mouse.

Maybe when I'm thirty,
I'll love to eat baked beans
I'll love to wear the colour pink
I'd wish I was in my teens.

Maybe when I'm thirty,
I'll have so many kids
I'll have to scrimp and save
I'll go around collecting bottle lids.

Maybe when I'm thirty,
I'll have a fantastic job
I'll get a new car every year
I'll cook spaghetti on the hob.

Maybe when I'm thirty,
I'll look after my mum
I could be living with my friends
Or I could become a chef, yum, yum.

Who knows what I'll be doing
When I'm thirty
I'll have to wait and see.

Lauren Chapman (11)
Archbishop Temple School

Cacklesbury Creepy Castle

Surrounded by a cluster of trees,
There's a place that's not locked with any keys,
It always rains there with wind and gales,
So you can't hear the ghostly moans and wails,
Leading up to the castle entrance is a winding path,
With gargoyles with faces like Aunt Cath,
The castle's there to make you shiver,
Enough to make a lion quiver.

Looming overhead, the ghostly door stands ajar,
Then a corridor with ancestors that date back far,
To the left is a door, dusty and old,
Behind it is a bat with eyes oh so cold,
Somewhere in the kitchen, a chain clinks
Musty mould grows on ancient sinks
The castle's there to make you shiver,
Enough to make a wolf quiver.

Coffins lie in creepy cellars, gathering dust,
In the attic there is a grim, eerie bust,
Spooky spectres and a grim ghoul,
Even more scary than going to school,
Dracula, bogey monster, the castle's got it,
It will drive you up the wall, bit by bit,
The castle's there to make you shiver,
Enough to make *you* quiver!

Mary Clayton (12)
Archbishop Temple School

Fire

Smoke alarms ringing,
Songbirds singing,
Raging through the city,
Without pity,
Fire!

Racing like a bird,
Hardly saying a word,
Burning through house after house,
Killing every mouse,
Fire!

Scorching all around,
Making a terrible sound,
Driving people mad,
Making the city sad,
Fire!

With the flames crackling
The city blackening,
Clouds everywhere,
Not one person stood to stare,
Fire!

Emma Worthington (11)
Archbishop Temple School

Escaped Tiger

Seven long years,
That's my age,
And all my life
I've been kept in a cage.

I stalk through London,
On this fine, summer's day,
I'm getting very hungry,
But I enjoy hunting my prey.

I see something,
What can it be?
I run and pounce
On this treat for me.

As I leave a trail of blood
Plus a few arms and legs
A zookeeper chases after me,
'Please come back with me,' he begs.

I roar back at him,
'Not on your nelly,'
He won't mess with me anymore,
Because he's in my stripy belly!

Martha Smith (11)
Archbishop Temple School

Death

The soldiers stand in quiet ranks
Wind howling through their armour
The call to arms had been met
With untamed fervour.

The order rang, 'Charge!'
And the men ran
The nervous archers raised their bows
And the air sang
The men of Anogg
Waiting for the storm
Waited for death.

The world was bathed in darkness
As the rain wet the rock
Red met black
And blood flowed with rain.

The men of Anogg
Black banners held up high
Fought on through the battle
Fearless till they die.

The mountain men
Armour as red as blood
Evil in their hearts
Fought for death.

And chaos ruled all!

Robert Newton (11)
Archbishop Temple School

The Thing Under The Kitchen Cupboard

Last Sunday after tea
When it was my turn to do the washing
I heard a creak, grumble and sigh,
Then after a minute again there came some groaning.

What can that be, I wondered for a while,
What is this noise I hear?
For just last month had the kitchen cupboard been checked,
For there was a leak then.

Now there could be no leak,
For then that had been seen to.
So very slowly I peeked in the cupboard,
There it was, the thing, the monster.

I did not tell a soul
About this big problem,
Then again I crept so slowly downstairs at midnight,
To have a little peek again.

There it was,
With its gruesome green body,
Its eyes as deep as blood
And its pointy, spiky back.

I asked where it came from,
It said a faraway country.
So then I led it into the garden
And slowly, very slowly, it crept into the deep dark bushes
With a trail of moonlight beside it.

Sima Patel (12)
Archbishop Temple School

My Family

I have a strange mum,
She burps out of her bum,
She plucks at her moustache and eyebrows,
She has smelly feet as brown as cows.

I have a strange dad,
Hair he has never had,
He sleeps for most of the day,
'Zzzzzzz,' he will say.

I have two strange sisters,
Faces with spots that look like blisters,
They watch MTV all day long,
Some days they even wear a thong!

I have a strange brother,
He makes noise like no other,
He always buys designer clothes
Even with the amount of money he owes.

I have a strange family,
Including my clown uncle Stanley,
Then again we all get along
And act as though nothing's wrong!

Almajane Blaylock (11)
Archbishop Temple School

Friends

Friends are always there for you
And that goes for me too.

Friends give you advice on clothes, make-up and hair,
They will always be the ones that care.

Friends will give you a helping hand,
Then we can make a friendship band.

Friends cheer you up when you're feeling low,
They will never turn against you and become your foe.

Friends invite you over for tea,
Pizza and chips especially for me.

Friends are people that you can trust,
So clothes shopping with them is a definite must.

Friends will never leave you behind,
Because they are lovely and also kind.

Friends give you laughs,
Especially in maths.

Friends will never get mad,
They will never treat you bad.

That's what makes them great,
That's why they're your *best mate!*

Priya Modasiya (11)
Archbishop Temple School

People

People are the greatest treat,
They are better than any sweet,
Some are big and very strong,
Others are weak and do much wrong.

Some are tall
And many small,
Others be thin,
Some long to win.

A few that lie are filled with deceit,
Others may have very big feet,
Some think they are very cool,
They treat all others like a fool.

Whoever you are, whatever you do,
Just remember, you be you.

Kristian Hensby (11)
Archbishop Temple School

If I Was . . .

If I was an element
I would be air
Cold and breezy
Refreshing and lovely.

If I was a colour
I would be orange
Bright and cheerful
Angry and sad.

If I were a Simpson
I would be Bart
Sly and devious
Clever and cool.

But I'm not, I'm me!

Joshua Rothwell (13)
Brookfield School

If I Were . . .

If I were a famous person
I would be Hugh Heffner
Living in a mansion
Loads of money
Even has a pool
Best of all he has the girls.

If I were a musical instrument
I would be a trombone
A jazzy sort of instrument
And it can get a party going.

If I were a colour
I would be yellow
A kind, gentle and cool colour
Mellow, bright like the sun.

If I were a time of year
I would be the summer
The season of the sun
Parties, fun, jumping
In the river, cool.

If I were a fruit
I would be a strawberry
Dipped in cream, mixed in berries
Sweet and juicy, tangy and soft.

But I'm not
I'm me!

Josh Danson (14)
Brookfield School

If I Were . . .

If I were an animal
I would be a dragon
Polite, but fiery
Gentle then roaring.
If I were a colour
I would be red
Warm but warning
Beautiful but dangerous.
If I were a fruit
I would be an apple
Lovely and juicy
Sweet and crunchy.
If I were a day of the week
I would be Friday
Activities and PE
Happy and relieved.
If I were a game
I would be a game of pool
Skilful and cunning
Colourful and precise . . .

But I'm not -
I'm me!

Robert Oakley (13)
Brookfield School

Computer

Brand new flatscreen
Latest circuitry
Cordless mouse
Windows XP . . .

No plug!

Cameron Leyland (13)
Brookfield School

You Don't Know You're Born

'You don't know you're born, you!
Computer, TV, video, DVD, toys,
Bike, skateboard, roller blades,
Latest phone and designer clothes
Mother to cook your tea
Dad to fish with, brother to fight with
Clothes ironed, holidays abroad.'
I don't know I'm born, me!

They don't care I'm born, me.
School full of harm
Bullied and imposed upon
Ignored and misused,
'Give us your dinner money!'
'Give us your tosh,'
Every day
Over and over . . .

Over and over . . .
I wish I wasn't born, me.

Stefan Smith (15)
Brookfield School

Prepositions

Without her lover she cries
Near his heart she clings
Between them lies a world
Beneath them is their lives
Next to that only death
Among the lilies she waits
Under love she only grieves
Over the half truths and lies
Inside her heals lost freedom
Beyond all, she hopes.

Grant Whillans (14)
Brookfield School

If I Were . . .

If I were a place
I would be Turkey
Hot and dry
Exotic and warm.

If I were an animal
I would be a butterfly
Pretty and delicate
Colourful and symmetric.

If I were a car
I would be a Manta
Fast and comfy
And roaring past cars.

If I were a planet
I would be the moon
Cold and empty
Lonely and peaceful.

If I were a plant
I would be a rose
Warm and pretty
Beautiful and sweet.

But I'm not
I'm me!

Anthony Lesley (13)
Brookfield School

Smoking

Brand new packet with cellophane on
Hidden behind the gym wall
Teachers all inside
Been desperate since last break . . .

No light!

Shea Holloway (12)
Brookfield School

Elephant

E lephants are big
L arge
E xtremely soft
P lodding
H eavy
A loof
N oble
T all.

Steven Macaskill (14)
Brookfield School

I'm Crazy

One day I went to the park
And I was skateboarding in the dark.

I was skating in the fog,
While walking my dog.

I went up a steep hill
And saw Winston Churchill.

As I went past the swing,
I saw Elvis, 'The King'.

My dog went down the slide
And there was Bonnie and Clyde.

Then I saw last night's treacle
And shouted, 'I see dead people!'

I rang my mum, I was dizzy and hazy
And I shouted down the phone, 'Mummy, I'm crazy!'

I ran to the doctor he said I was mental,
He also said I had very bad dental.

My mum asked, 'What are the symptoms that are making him tense?'
'I'm sorry Ma'am, he's got the sixth sense.'

Josh Knapton (12)
Colne Primet High School

As I . . .

As I ran
Up the stairs
As I dashed
Across the landing
As I grasped
Hold of the handle
As I pulled
Open the door
As I looked
In the room
As I picked
Up the pen
As I thought
About my poem

As I . . .

Rebecca Whitaker (12)
Colne Primet High School

Kennings

A meat eater,
A bed heater.

A nasty biter,
A cat fighter.

A flea keeper,
A ring leaper.

A crime buster,
A floor duster.

A mess maker,
A water shaker.

Put these together,
I'm a . . .

Sally Wilkinson (12)
Colne Primet High School

The Magic Box

(Based on 'Magic Box' by Kit Wright)

I will put in the box . . .
The flutter of a butterfly's wings,
A raindrop falling on a rose's petal,
A stomach turning rapidly.

I will put in the box . . .
A young heart beating softly,
The softness of a baby's skin,
The pattern of a newly grown leaf.

I will put in the box . . .
A beautiful feather from an ornate bird,
The black in a night sky,
White snow that covers mountains.

I will put in the box . . .
Fresh air that hits your face,
Waves from a huge ocean,
A pale cloud from way up high.

My box is fashioned from floating dreams covered with snow
Secrets in the corners you'll never know
And a liquid lid tied with a bow.

I shall dream with my box
Be sly like a fox
I will share secrets in my dreams
Shoot whispers like beams.

Tahrina Golding (12)
Colne Primet High School

Who Am I?

An electric appliance
A sound giver
An intelligent liver
A word processor
Who am I?

David Fishwick (11)
Colne Primet High School

It's Hallowe'en

It's Hallowe'en
You're in for a scare
The witches and wizards are coming
For a dare.

It's Hallowe'en
You're in for a scare
The cats and bats are here
All coming in pairs.

It's Hallowe'en
You're in for a scare
Their potions are nasty
And are full of dragons' hair.

It's Hallowe'en
You're in for a scare
Because magic is here
In the air.

It's Hallowe'en, you're in for a scare.

Jade Tattersall (12)
Colne Primet High School

My Wedding Day

It was my wedding day, I was getting married to my beloved wife.
It was the happiest day of my life.

We went away on our honeymoon
It was far, far away on the moon.

When we landed we saw some goats
Some aliens that saw us, came out to gloat.

We then went away to their home
Their house was as small as a little gnome's.

We said goodbye and went on our way
Back home we went to Summer Bay.

Henna Murad (12)
Colne Primet High School

My Box
(Based on 'Magic Box' by Kit Wright)

I will put in my box . . .
The sound of crunchy, golden leaves,
The colour of the blue sky in summer,
The silkiness of a baby's skin.

I will put in my box . . .
The sound of a mouse moving quietly through the town,
The chilliness of snow in winter,
The happiness of a baby's smile.

I will put in my box . . .
The clashing sound in a storm,
The colour of secrets never to be told,
The smell of soft cookies baking in the oven.

My box is fashioned from the shape of a cloud with an icy design,
With a lock made from an angel's wing,
The whole world is in my box
But kept in my mind.

I shall act in my box . . .
In a movie in LA
Go to a premiere in London
Then win an Oscar in Hollywood.

Toni Dey (12)
Colne Primet High School

Footballer Kennings

A crowd puller
A net grabber
A hurtful thing
A sad sin
Put these together
What am I?

James Smith (11)
Colne Primet High School

My Box

(Based on 'Magic Box' by Kit Wright)

I will put in the box . . .
The sea slapping the stones,
Warmth from my clothes
And the light from the sun.

I will put in the box . . .
The first day I met my friend
Bluest water from the deepest sea
And the scent from my humble home.

I will put in the box . . .
The rage of a roaring fire,
The cold from a frosty winter
And the breeze from summer.

I will put in the box . . .
The bright green from a leaf
Red from a bright rainbow
And yellow from the glistening sun.

My box is fashioned from dinosaur bones
And silver with snow on the lid
And diamonds in the corners
Its hinges are made from a hunter's finger joints.

I shall build in the box . . .
The tallest tower and the smallest house
With the best weather from the hottest house.

Mark Brennan (12)
Colne Primet High School

Just Mine

(Based on 'Magic Box' by Kit Wright)

I will put in the box . . .
The splashing of consistent waves,
The feeling of an autumn leaf,
The smell of spring blossom.

I will put in the box . . .
The golden yellow of autumn trees,
The early morning sun just peeping,
The seedling poking through the ground.

I will put in the box . . .
The blanket of white snow,
The smell of newly cut grass,
The crispy brown of fallen leaves.

I will put in the box . . .
Seagulls squabbling over scraps of food
Dolphins flipping out of icy water
A newborn horse trying to stand.

My box is made from abandoned shells
The deepest, darkest of all the hells
You might not find it
You might not see that everything in there
Is all for me.

I shall hide it here
I shall hide it there
You cannot find it
I do not care.
I shall run away, not tomorrow, but today
I do know where, but I cannot say.

Jamie Harvey (12)
Colne Primet High School

Kennings - The Rain

A puddle maker,
A hair wetter
A rust inventor
A jacket soaker
I tap on your windows,
When you are in bed.
What am I . . . ?

Rebecca Thompson   (11)
Colne Primet High School

What Am I?

I come from the ground
I shoot from all around
I stop your tellies
I rumble your bellies
I am coming out
I am coming to shout
I've come to scare you
Put these together,
What am I?

Naomi Coultas Ferns (11)
Colne Primet High School

Landfill

A rubbish disposer
A waste enclosure
A trash eater
A nature defeater
A rat base
An animal killer's mace
Put these together
What am I?

Byford Adlington (11)
Colne Primet High School

Storm

A rainy night
There's no birds in flight
The thunder's booming
The lightning's zooming
It has an eye
And it is in the sky
Put these together
I am a . . .

Abigail Hirst (11)
Colne Primet High School

What Am I?

Del Boy's chancer,
A butler's dancer
An industrial property
Think of Gary Doherty
A little boy's dream
Leads up to fame
Sweet and funny
I am *money!*

Freddie Bailey (12)
Colne Primet High School

Time

A time ticker
As fast as a flicker
As slow as a snail
But like a flick of a tail
Never enough of it
Never enough to sit
Put these together
What am I?
Time!

Sophie Holdsworth (11)
Colne Primet High School

My Magic Box

(Based on 'Magic Box' by Kit Wright)

I will put in the box . . .
the day I caught my biggest fish,
the night I finished the biggest book on my shelf.

I will put in the box . . .
the sound of the waves on my favourite holiday.

I will put in the box . . .
my dad's laugh,
the Big Dipper at Blackpool,
a swimming pool with loads of slides.

I will put in the box . . .
the smell of a vanilla milkshake,
the colour of my old fish's fish tank water.

I will put in my box . . .
the weather of Scotland and the weather of the British Isles.

Josh Hindle (13)
Colne Primet High School

Pen

This helps you write a story
A story full of glory
It's full of ink
It could be pink
All the types of these
Won't hold up your knees
When they all run out
They won't come if you shout
When you ask for one
They might have none
But you have got to ask
To do the task
Go look in the den
And you'll find my *pen!*

Ashleigh Lonsdale (11)
Colne Primet High School

My Magic Box
(Based on 'Magic Box' by Kit Wright)

I will put in my box . . .
the smile of my grandad,
the sound of my bird singing,
the light in the morning.

I will put in my box . . .
the sound of a motorbike,
the sound of my mum's friend.

I will put in my box . . .
the smell of rock being made,
the smell of candyfloss,
the colour of the moon.

I will put in my box . . .
my picture of my family.

My box is made of fine gold crystals, with moons on the lid.

Shaun Mullens (12)
Colne Primet High School

The Magic Box
(Based on 'Magic Box' by Kit Wright)

I will put in the box . . .
The swish of a small, silken dress on a mild summer morning
Fire from Bonfire Night, gleaming in the bright sky
With lots of noise and lots of colours
The tip of a necklace sparkling in the sky like a bright light.

I will put in the box . . .
The tip of a fire from the nostrils of a dragon
A person on a broomstick
And a witch on a white horse.

Toqir Hussain (12)
Colne Primet High School

The Magic Box

(Based on 'Magic Box' by Kit Wright)

I will put in the box . . .
The memories from Eid on a summer's night
Three violet wishes spoken in Giyarati
The sharp teeth of a Siberian tiger.

I will put in the box . .
A picture of the first smile of a baby
A diary with all my memories of my family
A last joke from my uncle.

I will put in the box . . .
My first day at school
A secret in each corner
And the colour of the sea.

My box is fashioned with gemstones
With stars on the side
I shall walk in the box
In the great Pendle forest.
The leaves swish around
The colour of the sky.

Sabrina Rahman (12)
Colne Primet High School

What Am I?

A book to tell
How to spell
A book to see
How easy it can be
Full of words
How absurd
Good to read
It's a good deed
Put them together
What am I?
The dictionary!

Lauren Kegg (12)
Colne Primet High School

The Magic Box

(Based on 'Magic Box' by Kit Wright)

I will put in the box . . .
the texture of a lion's fur coat,
the smell from the feet of a giant,
the tips of the fingers touching the door.

I will put in the box . . .
a painting full of different colours,
a smelly pig's pink ear,
the texture of a spider's skin.

I will put in the box . . .
the fierce sound of a tiger,
the sound of leaves swaying in the breeze,
and the smell of sweaty goo.

I will put in the box . . .
the coloured scarf of a snowman,
the texture of an elephant's trunk
and the smell of a piece of rotten cheese.

Suzanne O'Brien (12)
Colne Primet High School

Hallowe'en

Barney's teeth are so rotten
They're nearly dropping out
And if you see him late at night
Be careful not to shout.

Every dark and rainy Hallowe'en
When Barney comes around
He will hear someone scream
Because he's come to town.

Charlotte Connell (11)
Colne Primet High School

The Magic Box

(Based on 'Magic Box' by Kit Wright)

I will put in the box . . .
the petal of a yellow lily on a sunny day.
Soil from the plant pot of a young woman's leaf
patiently waiting to grow on the stem.

I will put in the box . . .
the green grass from a garden.
A picked flower from the corner bed,
a sunny sky to show the pride.

I will put in the box . . .
a footstep of a dinosaur.
A picture of the beach.
A necklace of the bride.

I will put in the box . . .
a feather from a peacock.
An arrow of love.
An engraved death.

Siân Simpson (13)
Colne Primet High School

Hallowe'en

He lives in a graveyard at night
Where nobody's ever seen
He tries to give you a fright
And he comes out at Hallowe'en.

His hair is grey and white
His eyes are blue as a ball
He walks out every Hallowe'en night
And he is five feet tall.

Simon Thornton (11)
Colne Primet High School

Magic Box

(Based on 'Magic Box' by Kit Wright)

In my magic box . . .
I would put my grandma's hug,
a dolphin singing in the air,
warm clothes, fresh out of the dryer.

In my magic box . . .
I would put in a snowy day in the middle of summer,
the smell of my mum's perfume when she goes past,
the colour purple when I am confused.

In my magic box . . .
I would put a picture of me and my family all together,
getting presents early in the morning,
and staying in bed as long as I can.

In my magic box . . .
I would put the smell of hot chocolate on a cold afternoon,
the colour of blue when I am sad,
In my magic box.

Chlôe Jane Savage (12)
Colne Primet High School

Hallowe'en

H ands that are like a pumpkin
A nkles that are like a skeleton's
L ong arms like a tree log
L ungs that are as good as a fish's
O nly the very, very brave
W ould mess around with him
E ating people for tea
E ven when he's not hungry
N ever eats the people that are his friends.

Andrew King (11)
Colne Primet High School

The Magic Box

(Based on 'Magic Box' by Kit Wright)

I will put in the box . . .
A sip of the most blue water from the most blue sea
Fireworks sparkling on a bright Bonfire night
A shark tooth, dripping in blood.

I will put in the box . . .
Scales of a rainbow fish
A treasure-chest full of gold
The sun burning hot as fire.

I will put in the box . . .
Lightning from an electric fish
A pyramid cursed with spells
And the first laugh of a baby.

I will put in the box . . .
A witch on a broomstick
A snowman melting away
A dragon's breath breathing fire.

My box is fashioned from ice to gold
With stars twinkling a secret code
Hinges of a giant's toe connected to a dinosaur.

My box shall surf across the great, wavy sea
Then land on a beach the colour of the sun.

Waris Ali (12)
Colne Primet High School

Hallowe'en Poem

Every Hallowe'en night he rings people's bells
Even though he is the zombie of Hell.
He waits for them to answer the door
When they answer the door he jumps on them
And makes them fall on the floor.

He's got messy grey hair and looks like a scary bear
He's got horribly bony legs and he likes eating lots of eggs.

Jamie Ingram (11)
Colne Primet High School

My Magic Box

(Based on 'Magic Box' by Kit Wright)

In my box I will put . . .
my favourite colour, I will put
my favourite book.

In my box I will put . . .
my rabbit's soft skin, I will put
the sound of people stepping on snow.

In my box I will put . . .
the soft, but cold feeling of snow, I will put
my best moment.

In my box I will put . . .
the pair of earrings my grandmother
gave me before she died.

In my box I will put . . .
the heat of the sun, I will put
the shining stars and I will put
my family's laugh.

Arooj Butt (12)
Colne Primet High School

Spirit Witch Poem

She lives in a haunted house
But she wouldn't scare a mouse
Her hair is long and white
Her skin is pale and bright
Her teeth are as white as milk
Her dress is made of silk.

She sits there all alone
And she doesn't have a phone
She has to talk to her cat
And eats lots of cakes, but doesn't get fat.

And that's the end of my tale today
Maybe I will visit her one day.

Sonia Rahman (11)
Colne Primet High School

The Magic Box

(Based on 'Magic Box' by Kit Wright)

I will put in the box . . .
A jumping spark from an electric plug
A cowboy on a rocket
And an astronaut on a black horse.

I will put in the box . . .
A tiger with a hungry belly
A litre of the finest water from the river Ouse
And a leaping stickleback.

I will put in the box . . .
A fiery dragon from China
A joke from my mate
And the first cry of a baby.

I will put in the box . . .
A claw of a tiger
A tongue of a snake
And the teeth from a crocodile.

My box is fashioned from
Plastic and steel and cardboard
With a moon at each corner
And smells of a rotten egg.

I shall fly in my box in the open great sky
The fly to the great yellow sun.

Chris Willett (12)
Colne Primet High School

The Magic Box

(Based on 'Magic Box' by Kit Wright)

I will put in the box . . .
The last words of a dying man,
Fire from a Bonfire Night,
The tip of a tongue touching a tooth.

I will put in the box . . .
The heat of the sun in summer,
A snowman melting slowly,
A witch without her hat.

I will put in the box . . .
The first step of a baby,
A pot of gold,
A piece of Mount Everest.

I will put in the box . . .
The colours of the rainbow,
A model of the first aeroplane,
A big diamond in the jewellers.

My box is fashioned from leather, gold and crystal,
With diamonds in the secret corners,
Its hinges are the links of a silver chain.

I shall fly in my box,
Over the mountains,
Then wash away the bad things,
The colour of the sky.

Umar Waqar (13)
Colne Primet High School

The Magic Box

(Based on 'Magic Box' by Kit Wright)

I will put in the box . . .
A sound of a wave,
A glittery star,
The blue sky up high.

I will put in the box . . .
The green grass swishing from side to side,
A leaf fallen from a tree,
A red, big apple just picked.

I will put in the box . . .
Raindrops fallen from clouds,
The heat of the sun,
The glaze of a star.

I will put in the box . . .
A sound of a snowflake,
A splash of a puddle,
A mountain full of snow.

My box is clean from rain, snow and dust,
With ice-cold weather and secrets all around its corners.
Its hinges are tied together with glass and bones.

I will skate, play and have fun in my box
With big buildings and high mountains
And then wash away the silky sand
And the colour of the sky.

Bethany Golding (13)
Colne Primet High School

Secret Box

(Based on 'Magic Box' by Kit Wright)

I will put in the box . . .
Angry waves crashing against jagged rocks,
The bright yellow sun from the morning sky,
A whistle from a small, fluffy bird.

I will put in the box . . .
The smell of a rose freshly picked,
The scorching sun at midday,
A soft piece of wool from a sheep's back.

I will put in the box . . .
A leaf in the middle of the autumn,
Some white snow from winter,
Some lush green grass from summer.

I will put in the box . . .
A smooth stone from the highest mountain,
Some fresh water from the longest river
And a plant from the biggest forest.

My box is made from bamboo and leaves
Covered in a coat of glass.
It's hidden in a rainforest
Up a high tree.

I shall find an adventure in my box,
In the rainforest it is hidden,
Then climb the tree
That is forbidden.

Alex Evans-Shaw (12)
Colne Primet High School

My Magic Box

(Based on 'Magic Box' by Kit Wright)

I will put in my box . . .
A coat of chicken-pox,
Paper that cannot tear,
The smell of a bear,
Beaming light,
Peace, and no one having to fight.

In the box there will be . . .
A sting from a bee,
The texture of something muddy,
And Zack, my buddy.
The words from a person who does not lie,
Some arms that fly.

Some of the things in my box are . . .
Never-drying tar,
The sound of a cow saying, 'Moo,'
And a lot of activities to do.
A familiar face,
And everlasting lace.

The box will be made of silver and gold,
And it has to be small as I was told,
With moments to cry inside,
Make moments of laughter's guide,
With the padlock shining in the sun,
The box will weigh a ton.

When someone finds it,
Their life will be lit
With happy moments
They're better than ornaments.

They will treasure the chest
So it won't become another quest.

These things are nice
Even for some mice.

Robert Thompson (12)
Colne Primet High School

The Magic Box

(Based on 'Magic Box' by Kit Wright)

I will put in the box . . .
The first time I won a personal CD player,
The time when my baby sister was born,
The first time she tried to stand up on her own.

I will put in the box . . .
The first time she could make up words,
The time when my cat was scratching the carpet,
The first time my sister put her arms out to me.

I will put in the box . . .
The first time I held my baby sister,
The time I sat on my cold sofa,
The first time I made some sticky jelly.

I will put in the box . . .
The first time I changed my baby sister's smelly nappy,
When I smelt my tea ready,
When I smelt my mum making me a coffee.

I will put in the box . . .
The colour green to remind me of my cat,
The colour red when I cut my finger with a pair of scissors,
The colour blue to remind me of my sister's eyes.

I will put in the box . . .
The sun to remind me of summer,
Snow to remind me of winter,
Hailstones to remind me of my sister chucking her toys.

I will put in the box . . .
My mini diary that my best friend gave me from Wales,
My necklace that I got for my birthday,
My baby sister's clothes to remind me how small she was
                                    when she was born.

Sigourney Millward (12)
Colne Primet High School

My Magic Box

(Based on 'Magic Box' by Kit Wright)

I would put in my box . . .
Pure white snow my brother and I played in,
The green sapphire out of my sister's favourite ring
And the smell of my mum's chicken casserole.

I would put in my box . . .
The softness of my cat's fur,
My old dog's limp when he walked,
And the bubbles that came from my fishes' bowl.

I would put in my box . . .
My friends' laugh from when we joke
And their tears when something goes wrong.

In my magic box . . .
I would put all my special memories and secrets!

Charlotte Stone
Colne Primet High School

Seasons

The sun is blazing,
Summer's raising.

Leaves are falling,
Autumn's calling.

The weather's freezing,
Water's breezing.

Birds are shouting,
Spring is sprouting.

There's no other reason,
They're all a season.

Warren Singleton (13)
Colne Primet High School

The Natural Box
(Based on 'Magic Box' by Kit Wright)

I will put in the box . . .
The sound of swooping wind over the brisk moors,
The smell of pure air lingering over a still lake.
The feel of lush green grass swaying in my soft hand.

I will put in the box . . .
The fresh colour of blue slate, which makes up a Cumbrian town,
The coldness of a natural skyscraper when at the summit,
The warmth of a small feeble mammal in his snug nest.

My box is made from . . .
The dense rock that makes up a sheer rock face,
The hinges are made from the greenest stems from the darkest,
deepest forest.
The lock is made from a soft feather from a vicious bird of prey.

The unusual thing about my box is
That only my eyes are truthful to it, and if it is deceived,
It will cast a spell over itself and then it will leave.

Billy Warren (12)
Colne Primet High School

My Favourite Animal

My favourite animal
Isn't a cannibal,
It lives in a field all day long,
And has a fairly long tongue,
All the way
From grey
To bay.
I love this animal,
That isn't a cannibal.
What is it?
It wears a bit.
Can you guess, Inspector Morse?
Yes that's right, it's a horse.

Keely Ashworth (12)
Colne Primet High School

Trouble

My stupid brother has got me in trouble,
I wish I had a clone or a double;
To take all his yelling and screaming and shouting,
But by the end,
It'll be a new trend,
For everyone in school to be pouting.

I have to run far away,
Because I cannot stay,
I'm really, really gonna get done,
It was a Friday night,
Everyone was tucked in tight,
But I was out showing my bum.

Now I've come back,
No food in my backpack,
And my brother's burst my bubble,
Oh great, not again,
I guess I'm now back in trouble.

Matthew Brooks (13)
Colne Primet High School

My Dog

My dog is a boy
Who loves his chewy toy.
We take him out every night,
Even when it isn't light.
I always take my dog to the park,
When he sees another dog, he will bark.
My dog is now nine
And he's still feeling fine.

Natalie Whitfield (12)
Colne Primet High School

My Magic Box

(Based on 'Magic Box' by Kit Wright)

I will put in the box . . .
the textures of a kitten playing with a soft ball of wool,
the colour turquoise to show a gentle wave lapping up on
a silky beach,
a natural autumn leaf flitting to and fro between the high-rise pine trees
that cover the landscapes of Scotland's finest forests.

I will put in the box . . .
the hustle and bustle of a small town in the chilly Andalucian
mountains,
getting down to a morning's work,
a lion stalking a young buffalo that thinks it's safe
until the final roar and, *bang*, the innocent is no more,
a taste of the finest truffle chocolate that melts on the tip
of your tongue.

My box is created with . . .
hinges of hard ice, when opened, a mesmerising blue light,
It is shaped in an ellipse made from the hardest diamond.

I shall walk a long walk in Scotland's finest countryside,
then I shall settle in a comfy corner of my box for a long night's sleep,
then go when I'm ready for the new adventures of tomorrow.

James Hirst (13)
Colne Primet High School

Photograph

We'll try it on the sofa,
We'll try it on the stairs,
We'll try it in the shower,
We'll try it in the bath,
Before you start to giggle,
Before you start to laugh,
All we'll try to do is take a photograph.

Kyle Pearson (12)
Colne Primet High School

My Magic Box

(Based on 'Magic Box' by Kit Wright)

I will place in my box . . .
the lost city of Atlantis,
the flow of a trickling stream
and the brilliance of the moon.

I will place in my box . . .
the glow of purest silver,
the patter of rain in a tropical storm
and the roar of the sea as it eats away the land.

I will place in my box . . .
the faint light of a star on a winter's night,
the smooth feel of a steel blade
and the battle for a red dawn.

I will place in my box . . .
the doomed charge of an outnumbered army,
the stubbornness of a friend
and the familiar creak of some stairs.

My box is fashioned from the true silver mithril,
the burning of a blood-red fire,
the hardness of a mountain,
the lock is of a golden cloud.

I shall fly around the world on my box,
there and back again.
I shall keep my box in a place most secret
that only I shall know.

Daniel West (12)
Colne Primet High School

The Magic Box

(Based on 'Magic Box' by Kit Wright)

I will put in the box . . .
The galloping of white horses on the top of waves,
The heartbeat of a frightened ghost,
The long golden hair of a mermaid.

I will put in the box . . .
The smell of an elephant's tears,
The lightning from furious thunder,
The flowers falling from a pink sky.

I will put in the box . . .
The necklace swaying from a poisonous frog,
The fragrance which a fairy uses,
The silver lining of a snowy cloud.

I will put in the box . . .
The hatred in an angel's soul,
The happiness a devil feels,
The ice turning into fire.

My box is made from wood and glitter,
It has whispers in the corners and three drawers,
Each releasing a dream.

I will keep my box in a bigger box
And an even bigger one
Until we get to the eighth box.
Each is guarded by spells and charms,
And a silver bat with red demon eyes watching.
I shall die in my box and haunt my enemies.

Kayli Morant (13)
Colne Primet High School

My Magic Box . . .

(Based on 'Magic Box' by Kit Wright)

I will put in my box . . .
the calm sunset from the deserts of Africa,
the smooth skin of a baby's face,
and the laughter of friends and family.

I will put in my box . . .
the sparkling dew from a new morn,
the amber leaves from autumn trees,
and the scent of freshly cut grass.

I will put in my box . . .
the tapping of rain on slate,
the chocolatey taste of soft ice cream,
and the saltiness of the sea.

I will put in my box . . .
the blues and whites of the sky,
the frostbitten plants from winter eves,
and the luxurious petals from a red rose.

My box is decorated in silk,
the softest found,
and I pamper the smooth suede,
of the exterior.

I will surround my box with . . .
sugar and spice and all things nice,
then I will eat the spice,
the spice of India.

Charlotte Branch (13)
Colne Primet High School

Family United

This tale I'm going to tell,
Has happened to many a child as well,
But in my heart I feel it's only me,
I'm lost and broken, it's changing me.
My mum and dad whom I love so
Have gone separate ways and left me low,
Every day I think of us together,
But my mum says this will never.
Does she stop and think of me?
I'm 12 years old, this is not meant to be,
From June to January I've never smiled clear,
My mum covered up the truth, I could see,
My dad didn't want to go, he wanted me,
Me always crying,
Mum always shouting.
When a porcelain doll got broken they used to glue it back together,
But when it comes to a broken heart and home,
It takes more than glue.
Maybe a piece of my mind, maybe that will fix it,
These words from the start won't end,
As my heart is broken and will not mend,
Until one day, if that will be,
We will all reunite and happy will be.
So my life is young and full of sorrow,
I wonder what life will bring tomorrow.
I hope and pray for my dear mum and dad
To reunite as I am sad.

Katy Martin (12)
Colne Primet High School

The Box Of Dreams

(Based on 'Magic Box' by Kit Wright)

I will put in my dream box . . .
The sweet smell of a scented red rose,
The softness of a white, fluffy cloud,
The seven wonderful colours from a rainbow.

I will put in my dream box . . .
A gold, shining star up in the sky,
A brown, crumbly mountain surrounding us,
A silent whisper of a shiny shell from the sea.

I will put in my dream box . . .
A bunch of the most colourful flowers,
A small bluebird whistling cheerfully,
The scorching hot sun, so bright and yellow.

I will put in my dream box . . .
The sound of crashing waves against boulders and rocks,
The golden leaves that have fallen off an old oak tree,
The touch of a soft, white, gentle feather, fallen from an amazingly
                                        soft and smooth dove.

My box is decorated with silent snowflakes and colourful flowers,
With golden leaves that cover the lid and dreams all around,
Its feather hinges are made of tiny, soft ballerina slippers.

I shall dance to the shining stars,
Twirl back down to the silent Earth like a feather, back into my box.

Salma Hussain (13)
Colne Primet High School

My Magic Box

(Based on 'Magic Box' by Kit Wright)

I will put in my box . . .

The cheer of the fans when a goal is scored,
And the feel of baby feet.
The smell of melted chocolate.

I will put in my box . . .

The yellow of the morning sun and the black of the night sky.
When I hear my cousin laugh,
Not to forget when Burnley win a match.

I will put in my box . . .

The rush of the sea,
When the snow starts falling,
And the shine of a star.

My box is fashioned from snowflakes, white, bouncing clouds,
From the night sky and crispy leaves.
It will be silk inside and full of memories.
When opened it will play '500 miles',
And the sound of the swaying sea.

I shall fly to the Atlantic with my box,
And leave it in the snow,
So one day someone will find it,
And my memories will live on.

Daisy Eve (13)
Colne Primet High School

The Magic Box

(Based on 'Magic Box' by Kit Wright)

I will put in my box . . .

The smile of a laughing baby
The song of an ancient band
Holding the hand of my dying grandmother

I will put in my box . . .

The food from the greatest banquet
A pet to play with when I'm old
A friend I can share my feelings with

I will put in my box . . .

The memories in my head
The energy I have as I'm young
The life I haven't had

I will put in my box . . .

The sun as bright as a light
A taste of extraordinary foods
To try something different

My box is black with a silver rim and a skull engraved in the lid
With a special base that never ends.

I shall live in my box forever!

Shane Goodwin (12)
Colne Primet High School

Harry Potter

Harry Potter is a great book
It's fun to read and fun to watch
First comes Harry Potter with his lightning scar
Next comes Dudley with his big appetite.

Cameron Biggar
George Tomlinson School

My First Day At School

It's hard to explain the way I feel,
A place unknown but is so real.
A soft voice welcomed me to the place,
I looked up to see a lady's smiling face.
I was led to a table which was covered with shapes,
A small girl said, 'Hi, I am Grace.
I am three but soon will be four,
I am not afraid anymore.'
I looked back down,
To give a frown
And I said, 'Hey,
It's a lovely day.'
I smiled once more,
There was a knock at the door.
It was my mum,
With a bunny in a box.
It was the same bunny as the one on my socks,
I loved that bunny.
And I got it on the day that was sunny,
I will remember that girl who said, 'Hey.'

Misbah Javed (12)
George Tomlinson School

Ice Cream

I rresistible
C reamy
E xcellent

C one
R aspberry
E xquisite
A nd
M outh-watering.

Emily McDaid (12)
George Tomlinson School

My Family

My family can be good or bad
When they are bad they make me mad!
When I get mad I can sometimes give cheek
I can also look in my sister's diary and have a little peek.

We play games together, laugh and joke
While my nana goes outside and has a smoke
Sometimes my sister tells tales on me
So when she does I slip tons of sugar in her tea!

My dad reads the paper twenty-four seven
When my mum has a bath, she thinks it's heaven
My dad is tall, my mum is small,
My smallest sister plays with a ball.

My sister goes out and plays with her mates
Sometimes she goes out and plays on her skates
I go and hang around with my mates
And we go to the bakery shop and buy a load of cakes!

That is everything I have got to say
There is one more thing, by the way
Every day, my family and I have a good time
This is why I am doing this rhyme!

Jamie Bergin (13)
George Tomlinson School

My Summer Garden

The bees are buzzing from flower to flower
The goldfish are glimmering while swimming in the pond
The birds are tweeting in the tall, green trees
The cats are sunbathing sleepily in the afternoon sun
The caterpillars sit eating away at the green leaves
The butterflies are fluttering over the gardens
The little children are playing in the bubble-filled paddling pool.

Laura Green (11)
George Tomlinson School

My Family

My family is fun.
My family is great.
My family is groovy.
My family is lovely.

My mum is top.
My dad loves pop.
My sisters are trendy.
My brother is moody.

My mum is called Shelley.
My dad is called Vinny.
My youngest sister is called Abigail.
My second oldest sister is called Vanessa.
My oldest sister is called Natalie.
Then my brother who is called Karl.

I live in a five-bedroomed house.
I have a front room and a back room.
I have a kitchen and a bathroom
And five bedrooms.
My house is really, really big.

Danielle Yates (13)
George Tomlinson School

My Family

My family is cool, they are great,
they're perfect in every way.
They're crazy and wild but I don't mind,
they make me feel special every night and day.

I love them so, they love me too,
they buy me presents like new expensive shoes.

They fill my life with happiness,
I love them, they made me!

Georgina Croft (12)
George Tomlinson School

Loved Or Lonely?

I used to be loved,
It was like a dove,
By my family and friends,
Love was through a lens.

Then something went wrong,
Now there's no song,
Now I'm alone,
Now it's a bone,
My life is miserable
Bored and ignored,
I need my love back,
I love you loads,
Wish I had a code,
Love is all.

Sally Jenkinson (11)
George Tomlinson School

What Am I?

I glide through the sea,
Singing my song,
I swim through the sea,
My friends along,
When I am singing my cheerful song,
All of my friends join along.

My nose is a bottle
Waiting to pop
My fins are restless
Waiting to swim.

I am endangered
Because of all fishermen

What am I?

I am a bottlenose dolphin.

Alicia Cahill (12)
George Tomlinson School

When Will?

When will the world end?
It could end next year
Imagine we could stop it
By flowers or even a tear

But that's never going to happen
It's going to end one day
People hiding in their lofts
What will the government say?

How will the world end?
Can we beg for lives to save?
As I'm speaking right this minute
We could die by a tidal wave

What will happen to us?
This tiny little Britain
Any country could wipe us out
By pressing the red button.

Anthony Townley (12)
George Tomlinson School

Sasha

D aft as a brick wall,
O range spots all over,
B ig as an elephant,
E xtremely fast like a cheetah,
R uff! Barking mad,
M ad as a mad hatter,
A nimals of the world,
N aughty as children,
S ometime sad, sometimes happy.

All these things are my wonderful dog Sasha.

Georgina Lees (11)
George Tomlinson School

Seasons

Spring is when the flowers are new,
It's when the lambs come out to play
And the grass is filled with dew.
Spring is a brand new day.

Summer is when the sun comes out
And the temperature is hot,
Lots of ice cream and lots of juice.
I like summer a lot.

Autumn is when the leaves go red
And when the coolness comes.
It's when the skies are grey, grey, grey
And we all get frozen thumbs.

Winter is when everything's covered in snow
And all the houses are white
And this big change of temperature
Will give us all a fright.

Georgina Brett-Edwards (11)
George Tomlinson School

Your Love

Your love is like a river flowing through your body,
Your heart is like a block of gold that will never break,
Your body is like a statue carved by angels,
And your love is never fake.

I hope we'll be together forever,
You're like a rare pearl,
I hope we'll never fall out,
Cos I'm your only girl.

You always make me smile,
You really make my day,
You buy me lots of presents,
And make me laugh in a funny way.

Kate Watson (11)
George Tomlinson School

Maths

This is a poem all about maths,
It is about symbols, numbers and graphs,
Algebra is very complex,
You add up a+b to equal 'x',
You try it on a piece of paper,
If that doesn't work, try a calculator,
All your lifelong paths,
You will end up using maths.

Olivia McDermott (11)
George Tomlinson School

Lightning

I light up the midnight sky with my flash,
You'll have to be quick to see me dash,
I stamp on houses and trample on oak trees,
I knock down walls every time I sneeze,
I travel the world leaving destruction in my path,
Everyone will suffer my wrath,
Thunder and rain are my best friends,
When I'm with them, our fun never ends.

Hannah Wright (11)
George Tomlinson School

Rain

I can cause a flood with a clap of my hands,
Or I can stretch my arms across different lands.
My water flows through streams, rivers, lakes and seas,
When I start to pour everybody frowns at me.
You can't last without me, can't last a day,
I can help you in every single way.
I can drum on top of your rooftops,
Or I can help to grow the farmers' crops.

Charlotte Cardwell (11)
George Tomlinson School

My Family

I have two or three brothers, they are the best
but sometimes they can be a pest.
1, 2, 3, they are coming for me and they annoy me.

My mum is the best but sometimes she can be a pest.
She buys me prezzies that are teddies.
Her eyes twinkle like stars.

My dad is a giant, he is the best,
but sometimes a pest but better than the rest.
He has grey hair that matches an elephant's skin.
He has brown eyes that sometimes are mean
but he is the best.

I have a dog that is a pest, no other than the rest.
He jumps, barks and bounces,
he catches mice and his name is Marley.

Jessika Knott (12)
George Tomlinson School

The Weather

The wind, the sun, the snow, the rain
Some of them can be a pain,
The wind can be like a powerful train,
Or it can be like a whistle, ever so plain.

The sun can be very bright,
And very hot at all of its might,
The snow is like a silky white,
And you can have a snowball fight.

The wind and rain could ruin your day,
It might be bad if it's a sunny May,
The wind, the sun, the snow, the rain,
Some of them can be a pain.

Lewis Eyres (11)
George Tomlinson School

Family

My family are great, they're always good fun.
They can be happy, they can be sad,
And they can be angry when I'm quite bad.

They sort out things at school
When I'm in trouble.

But when I'm this naughty
They still love me.

They'll love me always,
Me and my sister too,
No matter what we do.

Daniel Molyneux (12)
George Tomlinson School

Flowers

Flowers are pretty, flowers are nice
The colours are nice and bright
Even when the sun is bright they just grow and grow.
There are lots of colours like blue, orange, pink and red
All the different colours catch my eye and I just have to pick one
Maybe I will pick yellow, blue, pink or green,
Which one do you think I will choose?

Gabrielle Riley (11)
George Tomlinson School

As Quiet As Can Be

As *quick* as a cheetah having a race with a *Ferrari*.
As *silent* as a shark waiting for its *prey*.
As *quick* as a computer sending messages to *India*.
As *shocking* as lightning when *struck*.
As *cute* as a puppy when born.

Rahail Mehrban
George Tomlinson School

Bright Stars

Stars are bright.
Stars are light.
Stars are pretty and sparkly.

They shine in the dark sky.
Stars are big,
Stars are small.
Stars are everywhere in the sky.
Stars are bright.
Stars are light.
Stars are everywhere in the night.

Kirsty Hodgson (12)
George Tomlinson School

Red

Red as a rose.
Red as a top.
Red as blood.
Red as a door.
Red as a book.
Red as paint.
Red as a wall that is red.

David Brown (11)
George Tomlinson School

Love

I love my family,
I love my friends,
I love my dog,
I love everything around me,
And that's what makes me
happy.

Natalaie Gregg (11)
George Tomlinson School

Life

Life can be hard, not always fun,
but as night brings dark,
morning brings sun.
When life gets tough,
no one seems to care
just give me a hand,
and I'll always be there.

It's hard to explain the way I feel,
a place unknown but it's so real,
a welcome to the place,
will put me on a 'smiley' face.
A girl my age has me on the page,
never lets me down,
to give myself a frown.

Amy Dugdale (12)
George Tomlinson School

Frogs

Frogs jump
Frogs hop
Frogs are slimy
Frogs croak.

David Donlevy (11)
George Tomlinson School

My Mum

My mum is kind
My mum is helpful
My mum is beautiful
My mum is a childminder
My mum is 29.

Jacob Leach (11)
George Tomlinson School

My Potion

Poison, poison, kill her quick
die, die, die when my fingers click.

Eye of newt, toe of frog,
tiger's tooth and strangled dog.
Stir them round, mix it quick,
she might just turn into a toothpick.

Poison, poison, kill her quick
die, die, die when my fingers click.

Owl's wing, tiger's head,
very soon she'll be dead.
Frog's leg, tongue of a snake,
in the cauldron, boil and bake.
Lizard's legs, witch's mummy.
Stir it quick, nice and yummy.

Poison, poison, kill her quick
die, die, die when my fingers click.

Louise Maamoun (12)
George Tomlinson School

Rabbits

I like rabbits, they hop about,
They go around the garden.
We cannot catch them,
However hard we try,
They go nibble, nibble at the grass.

There are many types of rabbits
Like an angora that is fluffy,
A chinchilla that has silky, silver fur.
A brown rabbit that is a naughty boy.

Bunnies are so cute and they have different colours
Like a peanut-coloured bunny.
I love bunnies.

Katy Relf (12)
George Tomlinson School

I Love Ice Cream

I love ice cream,
It tastes great,
It tastes even better with my mate,
Eat it fast,
Eat it slow,
Eat it in the sun
And even in the snow,
It's scrummy, yummy
And good for your tummy,
I love ice cream!

Lucy Wheeler (11)
George Tomlinson School

Weather

In winter when the fields are white
I say this poem is for your delight.

Winter is here, summer has gone,
So put your sun cream away
And put your woollies on.

Travel somewhere new
Where you will find me too,
So look at the sky and it is so blue.

Laura Fletcher (12)
George Tomlinson School

Love

Love is in my heart and my desire.
Romance is true whether you
are new or old from
what I know. Love
is just so true.

Becky Pearson (11)
George Tomlinson School

War Has Started

War is a time of hatred with others
Even other people would lose their lovers

War is a time of bomb shelters and planes
Children would be evacuated on goodbye trains

Tears were shed and hearts they were broken
War had started because Hitler had spoken.

The Germans would come ready to attack
They would come with their weapons and never look back.

Now war is over, so now it's our turn
The Germans have lost so now they will learn.

Kirsty Tomlinson (12)
George Tomlinson School

Sweets

I love sweets,
They're all so very nice,
Marshmallows, flying saucers
And many more.
Fruit salads, black jacks,
Black and reds are just too nice for me.

I love sweets
I love to eat sweets
And there are so many more.
My brother eats much more than me
Because he goes to the shop nearly every day.

Jordan Sharrock (12)
George Tomlinson School

Dogs

Dogs come in all different shapes
Colours and sizes too
Puppies and poodles
Great Dane to Dalmatian
Cocker and springer spaniel too

All dogs look nice, girl or boy
If you give them a treat
Savoury or sweet
Their hearts fill with joy.

Robert Gergus (12)
George Tomlinson School

Sleeping Draught

Stir the cauldron round and round
until the mixture's thin not thick
add the ingredients to make the sleeping draught.

Tongue of meerkat
leg of lizard
round and round the mixture goes
add the nail of the grim's foot.

Daniella Wardle (12)
George Tomlinson School

Cars

Cars go slow,
cars go fast.
Sports cars are my favourite,
they go really fast,
they go faster than you think.
But when they crash you're in trouble.

Aaron Rangeley (11)
George Tomlinson School

The Deep Blue Sea

Early in the morning
While I was having a shave
I looked out of the window
And I saw a very big wave
I walked up the shore
So I could see more
The atmosphere was heavy with salt in the air
There were lots of seagulls flying everywhere
This is the place I want to be
This is the only place for me
The deep blue sea.

Nic Caldwell
George Tomlinson School

Cheeky

There is a bird,
A bird called Cheeky,
If you get close it will scream,
And it goes right through you,
So don't get too close,
If you do it will bite as well,
So be quiet,
You are cute,
But you are noisy,
So please be quiet,
Thank you.

Thomas Webster (12)
George Tomlinson School

The Telly

Wow, I love the telly.
I watch it when I'm filling my belly.

I can use it for a video.
At eight I will do so.

I play on the computer till four.
Then, lately, maybe for a bit more.

And best of all are the cartoons
With the people that act like baboons.

It's good when I need
A few things to do.

By the way, I have a sister called Kelly
And that concludes the telly.

Jack Thompson (12)
George Tomlinson School

Miss Hughes

Oh Miss Hughes,
How we all love Miss Hughes.
She brightens up our day when she smiles.
Oh how we all love our teacher, Miss Hughes.
She's so funny, she brightens up the room.
Oh how we want to be like her!

Miss Hughes, Miss Hughes,
How we all love Miss Hughes.
She's not only our teacher but our dear friend too.
If there was a test for being simply the best
She would outshine the rest as the best.

Kelly Fairhurst
George Tomlinson School

She Makes Me Smile

The branches snap
as I walk along the ground.
Finally I reach the soil,
it's soft and mushy
under my feet.

I can see the trees
leaning over and hugging me,
caring for me lovingly,
the smell of grass
floating round in the icy air,
burning my nose.
The bitter taste in my mouth.

I bend over and push aside the leaves
that cover my treasure.
They are brittle and cold.
They start to freeze my fingertips.
Why am I here?

I see the name.
The one I am looking for.
The sun shines down
lighting up the golden words.
A smile creeps upon me . . .
there she is.

Sarah Newsham (15)
Hornby High School

War Is Like . . .

War is like brother fighting brother
War is like parent fighting parent
War is like family fighting family
War is like country fighting country
War is madness, why won't it stop?

Madeleine Larmour (13)
Hornby High School

Dolphins Leap In The Sunset

Sunset starts in a deep yellow colour,
Making all desperate hearts warm,
Fish swimming in the lonely sea,
Swimming in a deep, dark way.
Suddenly a bright blue spark arrives,
Bright as a glowing sapphire,
The *dolphin* is here!

Sunset starts in a fantasy orange colour,
Transmitting squeaks to another streak,
The dolphin swims to its new feeding ground,
More dolphins come squeaking and singing
Their sweet melodic song,
Leaping into the sunset, their smooth skin glistening.

Sunset sleeps in a blood-red blanket,
Smoothly diving into the sea,
Together they feed,
Together they return,
To home waters!
Sunset sleeps in a blood-red blanket.

Hannah Greene (11)
Hornby High School

Hurricane

Twisting, twirling, spinning round
People screaming, shouting.

Cows flying through the air,
Screeching cars start to slide,
Skidding everywhere.

Lorries flying round and round
In the howling hurricane.

Rebecca Mackay (11)
Hornby High School

Animals

Bears come with different coloured fur,
Black and white,
Which you can see through the night,
Brown and grey,
Which you can see through the day.

Dogs come in different sizes.
Big and petite,
Which you see when you eat,
Skinny and fat,
Which you see when the night turns black.

Cats eat different kinds of foods
Turkey or chicken flavoured food,
Which they eat when they're in a good mood,
Gravy that is lumpy,
Which they eat when they are grumpy.

Cows come with different patterns on their fur,
White with black spots,
When they are hot,
Just brown without anything else on their skin,
When they just had a din.

Foxes all hunt different things,
Rabbits and deer,
When they've remembered their fears,
Rats and mice,
When they are being nice.

Animals are unique in their own different way,
And hopefully that is how it will stay.

John Dean Elsworth (11)
Hornby High School

Wild Animals

Bears and whales,
They make no difference
Neither does the African elephant.

Jaguars, bobcats,
Are all a kind of cat,
Tigers are the cats with stripes.

Dolphins, whales,
They need water to survive.

Mooses are those weird things,
With those big antlers.

Llamas are creatures with long legs,
But they run too fast.

Falcons with those sharp, pointy beaks,
Flying through the sky chasing food.

The great white shark,
The master of the sea.

The blue whale,
The biggest in the sea,
Swims over six miles a minute.

Dolphins, the friendliest things in the sea,
Playing and laughing all day long,
Spinner dolphins,
Spotted dolphins,
I don't really care!

Laura Hearsey (11)
Hornby High School

Trafford Shopping

New Look . . .
Miss Selfridges . . .
Fusion . . .
And Top Shop . . .

Oh no, there's so many to choose from,
New Look is great,
Miss Selfridges is generous,
Fusion is gorgeous,
And can't forget glamorous Top Shop.

New Look,
Miss Selfridges,
Fusion
And Top Shop,

Let's not forget the amazing shoe shops.
Faith has the most attractive shops.
Faith has small shoes, big shoes and flat shoes.
Let's not forget the 'girls'-night-out' shoes!

Lorelle Bell (13)
Hornby High School

You Are Just Like Me

Why don't people see
You are just like me?
You and I have the same insides,
But you choose to eat me!

Splashing around in the sea,
You are just like me.
We do the same,
But why do you catch me?

Take my chicks away from me.
You are just like me.
Running around,
But why do you cook me?

Victoria Parker (13)
Hornby High School

My Friend Lorelle

My friend, Lorelle, was a very pretty girl
I had all the things in the world
Until she went away.

I see her every night in my mind,
Oh, why has she gone so soon?
I miss you Lorelle, every day and night
And you still give me a fright
To see that you're gone forever.

Samantha Jordan (13)
Hornby High School

Love Is Like . . .

Love is like a rainbow,
You'll never find its end,
Love is like a boomerang,
You'll always get it back,
Love is like a cherry tree,
You'll watch it grow a little more each day,
And then you'll see it bloom.

Laura McKeown (14)
Hornby High School

Crocs And Snakes

Crocs and snakes, they snap around
with fierce or venomous frowns.

Snakes, they slither around with their tongues sticking out
with their deadly bite waiting about.

The crocs are the same, but no venom here,
the crocs are silent until they're hungry.

The crocodiles bathe in the sun during the day
while they hunt, their meal is hanging around.

Abigail Atkin (12)
Hornby High School

Why Should I Be Famous?

Why should I be famous
when all my friends are dead
and
all I got was a beating about my head?

Why should I be famous,
my school used to be a house of love,
and taught us about peace, the white dove
but
why my school
and
why my friends?

Why should I be famous
when all my friends are dead
and
all I got was a beating about my head?

Annemarie Stevens (13)
Hornby High School

Two Days Of Terror

For two days I stood there
At school,
Men all around us,
Waiting,
Waiting to kill us,
Why did it happen?
My friends are gone,
I am alone,
Forty days have gone since I escaped,
Forty days of mourning have gone.

Amy Graham (13)
Hornby High School

We All Love Food

We all love food
Whatever the mood
Men like meat
Children prefer sweets

We all love food
When we're in the mood
A tasty Chinese
Or pie and peas

We all love food
If we're in a bad mood
Some steamy fish
Or fresh fruit in a dish

We all love food
So get in the mood
Give yourself a treat
Have something good to eat.

Ryan Oldfield (12)
Hornby High School

Who's My Friend?

Brown hair, brown eyes,
My friend's a big surprise.

Very tall, very smart,
My friend is good at art.

Long hair, very funny,
My friend is never clumsy.

Neat writer, very kind,
My friend is hard to find!

Bethany Gill (11)
Hornby High School

Dogs

Barking
Growling
Licking
Biting
Chomping
Running
Feeding
Sniffing
Howling
Cuddling
Waking
Struggling
Furry
Bad
Old
Dogs!

Tom Harris (12)
Hornby High School

Dolphins

Smooth, shiny,
Small, tiny,
Silently glides,
Cleverly hides,
Leaping, playing,
Water laying,
Can jump,
But don't have a lump.

Hanna Sill (12)
Hornby High School

Cats

Cats are nice
Cats are cute
Cats have furry ears
Cats are soft and very smooth
And have rough tongues.
They are very small
And can be nasty.

Arthur Lankester (11)
Hornby High School

Schooldays

Chairs clattering,
Teachers chattering,
Pens writing,
Pupils fighting,
School rules,
Swimming pools,
Bell goes,
We hear roars!

Leanne Ashcroft (12)
Hornby High School

Sudan - Haiku

Death, fear, genocide,
Bloodbath, starvation, beating,
Slaughter, destruction.

Theodor Ensbury (12)
Hornby High School

Hurricanes

Howling winds start to rise.
Screaming rivers beginning to die.
The twisting hurricane.

Screaming cars start to slide.
Dogs, frogs, cats and rats.
The roaring hurricane.

If you had the chance you'd run.
But the twisting hurricane
Gets closer and shakes you away.

What has the world come to?
The weather, the streets, the buildings,
The clouds die down,
The mighty hurricane goes
But there is only a quarter of the world left.

Nicole Keeping (11)
Hornby High School

Sharks

Scourges of the sea
Terrors of the ocean
Wild and dangerous hunters
Strong bites
Curious bites
Extremely fast and silent swimmers
Hunger and curiosity dominate
Young and lonely
Have fast families
You have to be careful or they will bite you.

Daniel Larmour (12)
Hornby High School

The Dreaded Liquorice Stick

The slimy, black, skinny bodies,
Of the dreaded liquorice stick
The stomach-turning flavour,
Truly makes me sick.

The oozing, gooey texture,
That you get inside your mouth.
I'd rather eat a poisoned frog,
Or a rotten, stinky mouse.

The blackened, sickly layer,
That I get upon my teeth,
It makes me want to bury it,
Into the ground beneath.

This substance that makes me hum
Some people love so much,
It's the one and only 'so-called' sweet
That I will never touch.

Jay Minuti (12)
Leyland St Mary's RC Technology College

The China Doll

A china doll sits on a toyshop shelf . . . waiting for a friend.
A little girl comes rushing in,
But opts for a clown that can bend.

A china doll sits on a toyshop shelf . . . waiting to be bought.
A boy comes in and looks at her,
But doesn't give her a second thought.

A china doll no longer sits on a toyshop shelf
Watching other toys bought instead.
Because she was bought just yesterday
And is now snuggled up in her owner's bed.

Laura Bolton (13)
Leyland St Mary's RC Technology College

I'd Love To Be A . . .

I wish I was a chocolate bar,
Ripple, Dairy Milk, a chocolate star.
I'd love to be a Dairy Milk,
touches your throat and turns to silk.
I'd love to be a king-sized Flake,
they taste so nice for goodness sake!
I'd love to be a large Crunchie,
I do believe they taste so munchy.
I'd love to be a giant Mars,
where all my friends would be chocolate bars.
I'd love to be a tasty Twix,
we would be eaten in quantities of six.
I've love to be a delightful Snickers,
when eaten, people would lick us.
I wish I was tasty and yummy,
I'll just have to feel the sensation in my tummy.
I wish I was a chocolate bar,
Ripple, Dairy Milk, a chocolate star.

DJ Beswick (12)
Leyland St Mary's RC Technology College

Silence!

Every day at twelve o'clock,
The teacher would come in and say,
'Shush, silence, quiet,
Or it's detention at break today!'

At the start of every lesson,
She tells us not to shout,
But she doesn't even know,
What we are talking about.

We could be discussing Shakespeare,
We could be discussing good books,
We could be discussing biology,
Or how Peter Pan beat Captain Hook!

Christopher Coulson (12)
Leyland St Mary's RC Technology College

The Fungle With The Small Nose

Once upon a forest,
Far beneath the trees,
There lived a small but happy clan,
And in this clan there was one fungle,
The fungle with the little blue nose.

The fungles would tamper and tinker and toil,
All day they would work in the sun,
But this one little fungle,
With a little, small nose,
Would sit in his house and cry.

The fungle wouldn't work,
No toiling for him,
As he cried many buckets all day,
And when all the fungles would come back to bed,
This fungle would go out to the well.

He would look down into the well,
And that would set him off crying again,
As he wished he could leave and get away,
He would travel all over to find his love,
The Gorgie with the fluffy pink hair.

He wanted to see her,
And give her the news,
Of how he wanted to travel the world with her,
And all those fungles just tinkering all day,
Would stare at him as he bid them goodbye.

So . . .

In a very big forest,
Far beneath the trees,
There lived a small but happy clan,
And in this clan there was one fungle,
Who left and found his love.

Megan Walters (12)
Leyland St Mary's RC Technology College

The Sound Of Silence

I sit here in the dead of night
Alone, but not afraid.
For my friend is here beside me.
Always there when I listen
Sometimes I can hear her whisper back
I will never be alone when I listen to
The sound of silence.

I am left deserted in a faraway land
But my friend is still with me.
She will walk with me to the edge of the world
I will never be lonely with her at my side
She will still be here when the world ends
I will never be alone when I listen to
The sound of silence.

The fire is burning in the grate
I am sitting around with my friends.
She is among them
She whispers occasionally
But most of the time she just sits and listens
I will never be alone when I listen to
The sound of silence.

Cecilia Brown (12)
Leyland St Mary's RC Technology College

'P'

Food is a matter of letter to me,
In that everything I like begins with 'P'.
My starter of course would be Pâté of duck,
Or goose in fois gras, and happily I'd tuck
Into large portions with French bread and butter
No sorry, not butter, that must be 'Putter'.

For main course, fish is the dish of the day,
Served with prize Potatoes, Peas and Parsnips, they
Are my favourite when roasted and steaming hot
As the chef brings them out, all fresh from the pot.
So fish and veg arranged, a culinary art
Everything in its 'Plaice' and all good for the heart.

And now to dessert, 'Postre' in Spain,
Pomegranates, Peaches and Pears from our lane.
Many 'P's make the perfect end to a meal -
Pineapples and Pastries, the choice, an ordeal
Of colours and flavours, texture and smell,
So choosing in a restaurant for me is hell.

Natural or psychological, 'P's are my thing.
The produce of paradise fit for a king.

Victoria Butler (12)
Leyland St Mary's RC Technology College

Our World - Hope Or Despair?

In some countries there is bombing,
Tragic deaths
And people sobbing.
In other countries, people shot,
Others left alone to rot.
In different places there is crime,
Grannies mugged, not a nice time.
This is despair - no one cares.
But there is hope.
Children get an education,
Ready for their next step along the road.
Diseases are cured, more people are healthy.
We still have hope, both poor and wealthy.
Just remember, don't be sad,
For our world is not that bad.

Dominique Harrison-Bentzen (12)
Leyland St Mary's RC Technology College

Motion

Into the sunshine full of light,
Leaping and flashing, morning till night.
Into the moonlight, whiter than snow.
Waves like flowers when the wind blows.
Into the starlight, rushing in spray.
Happy at midnight, happy by day.
Ever in motion, blithesome and cheery,
Still climbing heavenward, never weary.
Glad of all weathers still seeming the best.
Upward and downward motion thy rest.

Jessica Illsley (12)
Leyland St Mary's RC Technology College

A Recipe For Happiness

Throw in the sun
And we'll all have fun.
Add a rabbit, or maybe two
What to add next; give us a clue.

Chocolate, biscuits and sugary snacks
Put in some crisps, just a couple of packs.
Drop in a little dog
Don't get anything out of the bog!

Put in a smile
Warm water from the Nile.
Add in drops from the rainbow
You won't be feeling low.

Now we'll mix the solution round
Take your thoughts off the ground.
So that is it, you won't be sad
Take a sip and you'll be glad.

Louise Hendy (12)
Leyland St Mary's RC Technology College

Death

Where do we go when the juice is gone?
Where do we go when the light has shone?
What does one's ethereal self become
When all the deeds in life are done?
Do we become a transparent ghost
Or go the place we hate the most
Or find a time where pleasure grows
Or go by a thing that nothing knows
Or is there a sense never seen
Or do we just

Die?

Marcus Webb (14)
Little Lever School (Specialist Language College)

From A Boy To A Man

The players marched out one by one,
In third place was their new son,
Even though his shirt was torn,
It was better than the blue that he had worn.

He chased and raced but to no avail,
But you knew one time he wouldn't fail,
On seventeen Ruud slipped him through,
Without any worries he knew what to do.

Once again United attacked with pace,
A chase for Giggs, he won the race,
He looked up and passed to the beast,
He slotted it in, there's two at least.

He marched in, smile on his face,
He knew they thought he was ace,
63 minutes, free kick on the 18-yard line,
He knew one more and the ball was mine.

The United players said, 'It's yours Wayne,'
He struck the ball as fast as a plane,
It hit the net, this was Rooney's day,
Distraught on the ground, the keeper lay.

The manager thought, *what a debut!*
Not forgetting the score was 6-2.

Jamie Gordon (15)
Little Lever School (Specialist Language College)

Poetry

P oetry is horrifying, always a bad dream,
O nly for once a year, forever it will seem.
E very time I think about it, I wonder if it's right,
M ust I really whinge about it and put up such a fight?

Alexander Clarkson (13)
Little Lever School (Specialist Language College)

Make A Difference

Give them food
Stop the poverty
Treat them the same
It's called equality

Every colour
Every creed
There is someone out there
Someone in need

Will you help
Or just walk by?
Stop the tears
You decide

Make a difference
As a community
After all
We are one, big unity.

Catherine Doyle (14)
Little Lever School (Specialist Language College)

Feeling Depressed

D amaged confidence and thoughts.
E choing around my bloodshot eyes.
P ushed into a suffocating awake sleep.
R ivalry between my smiling eyes and my cold heart.
E ventually this will go, won't it?
S topping the tears from eroding your face.
S leep I want to but can't.
E verything so upsetting.
D own, down I go, falling into a pit of drowning sorrow.
   Overpowering in its arrival.

Rebecca Bradbury (15)
Little Lever School (Specialist Language College)

Did He Know?

As I climbed into the back
Of what they called the 'family car' at funerals,
I cast my mind back
To a girl showing off her engagement ring
He was all smiles for me
But did he know then?

A year flies by, he guides me down the aisle
A girl in a white dress with red roses in her blonde hair.
We were all smiling,
But did he know then?

The car started. My mother began to sob.
My husband held me close.
An old man took his hat off in the street.
My mother's sobs increased. He held me closer.

Three months ago we told him about our baby.
He knew about his cancer then.
He never told us he would never live to see his grandchild.
But, did he know?

Bethany Heslop (14)
Little Lever School (Specialist Language College)

Goodbye Friend

She's gone now, maybe in a better place now,
Will I see her again? Who knows? Maybe some day,
I wish she still lived with me.
Her wet nose, her floppy ears,
Her flabby cheeks and silky fur.
Will she be back? Who knows? Who knows?
Every night I look up at the stars
I see a dark and happy face, she's saying,
'Goodbye my friend.'

Matthew Laisby (12)
Little Lever School (Specialist Language College)

Sunday, 2nd October

12.04am
The sun retires for another night
And passes the baton to the moon once again
The moon takes the responsibility with pride
And shines as bright as a thousand candles
A gradual silence falls over the city
As if taking the hint from the perpetual nature
The darkness descends through the streets
Leaving one light to shine for all
Reflections glimmer off the damp sea of grey
And a whole new city stares back at its elder
A light mist fills the once empty spaces
And the cold remains incognito
The curtains are drawn
And the night is shut away
But the streets are not empty
Though the hour is late
Because when one world sleeps
Another awakes
And so the moon retires for another day
Passing the baton to the sun once again.

Sunday 2nd October
7.07am.

Kendall Holland (15)
Little Lever School (Specialist Language College)

Friends

Some people think friends are like targets,
That you aim for every day,
But I think you are the arrow that guides me in every way.
That's why you're so special
That's why you're my best friend,
And I hope and I wish and I know
You won't dis that I'm with you right to the end.

Rebecca Payne (14)
Little Lever School (Specialist Language College)

Seasons

Spring,
This is the season for all that's new,
This is the season where wedding bells ring,
This is the season where daffodils grow,
This is the season of spring, you know.

Summer,
Oh what a glorious season;
The sun is shining, the kids are playing,
We all love summer for its dazzling sun,
You do know this is summer.

Autumn,
Red, yellow, brown leaves,
Rain, rain, rain and even more rain,
Now the hibernation starts,
This is all in autumn.

Winter,
Snow, hail, sleet and more rain,
Christmas is drawing near,
All the children look forward to it,
They've been waiting all year,
Winter's now over,

The chain starts again.

Ross Hampson (14)
Little Lever School (Specialist Language College)

Cats

Cats sit there all innocent during the day.
Night-time comes and they are off in a devilish way.
Fighting and hissing whilst we sleep,
Daytime comes and they are suddenly sweet,
Curled up on the sofa fast asleep.
Night-time comes and off they set,
Fighting and hissing, oh what a pet!

Laura Hinchliffe (12)
Little Lever School (Specialist Language College)

A Poem About Basketball

Basketball is a fast-paced game
The NBA is its name,
The players are very tall,
Look cool when dribbling the ball
Up and down the court they go
Shooting, passing, dribbling
They've just lost the ball, oh no!
Now the other team's got possession
So much anger and aggression
Passing to a teammate
The defender gets there, too late
He puts up the shot, it looks grim
Rolls around the rim and out
There are seven seconds to go
Through the legs, round the head
Shoots, victory! There you go
With 0.01 seconds to go.

Niall Berry (11)
Little Lever School (Specialist Language College)

Swimming

I enjoy swimming
Especially if I race
I zoom off quick
I keep my pace

When I get into the water
I begin to swim
I get faster and faster
Eventually I win

Also I like to play water polo
Water polo is a water game
Normally our team wins
And most people cheer my name.

Thomas Gleaves (11)
Little Lever School (Specialist Language College)

The Garden Of Life

The rose so sweet and tender
Although it seems to be.
Amongst the thorny stem
There hides
A flower that seems to plea.

The daisy is small and petite
With petals as white as snow.
The centre like a tiny moon
It's now
A flower that needs to grow.

The tulip, tall and majestic
Bathing in the sun.
It stands so tall and proud
Waiting until . . .
A flower's life is fun.

Vicky Horrocks (12)
Little Lever School (Specialist Language College)

My Hero

The Wanderers are brilliant
The Wanderers are good,
The players do their best,
And play like good footballers should.

In good weather and in bad,
With our season tickets, me and my dad,
Are always at the game,
Calling out our favourite names.

'Jay-Jay, Jay-Jay,' I shout very loud,
'Come on, give us a goal.'
Then when the game is over,
And the Wanderers have won,
My dad and I are on our way home,
'What a great game you missed, Mum.'

Michael MacArtney (11)
Little Lever School (Specialist Language College)

Little Angel

As people gather and say, 'Goodbye,'
the street seems to stand still.
Even the bees have stopped their
everlasting 'buzz'.

All you can hear is the sound of
tiny tears seemingly thumping onto
the floor, like a giant's feet.

When they bring in the terrible wooden
box, we see the angel whose smile
always warmed the coldest of hearts.

Poems are read about how
she coped with her asthma.
Her football team serenades her,
they will never be the same.

Eventually the terrible day comes to an end.
Although she will never be forgotten.
We all loved her so much.
That little angel.

Sarah Robinson (16)
Little Lever School (Specialist Language College)

My Cat

My cat is a fat cat,
A smart cat,
A nasty cat.

My cat is a lazy cat,
A slow cat,
A sly cat.

My cat is a black cat,
A green-eyed cat
And her name is Pawsha.

Daniel Manton (12)
Little Lever School (Specialist Language College)

Football

Kick the ball,
Flick the ball,
Whack the ball,
Smack the ball,
Do whatever you want with the ball.

Throw the ball,
Toe the ball,
Save the ball,
Do the Mexican wave with the ball,
Do whatever you want with the ball.

Head the ball,
Thread the ball,
Bend the ball,
Send the ball,
Do whatever you want with the ball.

Jake Melling (12)
Little Lever School (Specialist Language College)

The Witches' Cauldron

Into the deep, dark, black pot,
Goes some hair tied in a knot.

Add the entrails of a lark,
Now the heart of a shark.

Throw in the skin of an eel,
Toss in the eyes of a seal.

All the witches stand in a circle,
Last ingredient is the shell of a turtle.

The potion bubbles and curdles,
As the witches cackle and gurgle.

Grab a spoon and stir it well,
Now you've made a magic spell.

Jennifer Francis (11)
Little Lever School (Specialist Language College)

Autumn

Autumn is here
Conkers crashing on the ground
Children playing all around
Every night cold and dark

Autumn is here
Animals are hibernating
All the trees are bare
All the weather wet and windy

Autumn is here
Murky water
Catching colds
Drinking hot drinks
It's cold, cold, cold

Autumn is here
Brown leaves on the ground
Rain dropping all around
Hedgehogs scurrying all around

Autumn is here
People sitting in the house
Watching telly all day long
Autumn is here.

Victoria Lammas (11)
Little Lever School (Specialist Language College)

The Man

One day as I watched TV,
I thought that I could see,
A man three inches tall,
Who was totally bald,
And he sat there staring at me.

Joshua Marland (13)
Little Lever School (Specialist Language College)

My Room

The pale, painted purple and blue walls,
(separated in the middle,
like the once apartheid nation of South Africa)
enable me privacy and a home for my belongings.

Bunk beds are erected in the corner,
as if they are soldiers at Buckingham Palace.
And the wardrobe and chest of drawers
are an old, married couple,
standing by each other no matter what.

Two guinea pigs lie peacefully in their cage,
unaware of the horrors of war and famine.
Their strong odour fills the emptiness around them.

But it's not what's inside my room that matters,
it's the fact it belongs to me.

Caroline Kearney (15)
Little Lever School (Specialist Language College)

Another Season

Another season has passed
And autumn time is here
The leaves are falling to the ground
It's my favourite time of year

The weather is changing
The nights go colder and dark
The fallen leaves are everywhere
Especially in the park

It's good to be indoors
When it's windy, rainy weather
By the fireside nice and warm
All the family together.

Hayley Johns (11)
Little Lever School (Specialist Language College)

A Poem For A Competition

Think of a poem
Fit for a competition
Head in a whirl
And no clear vision

Should it be happy
Or should it be sad
Or should it be about me
A typical lad?

My brother, my mother
Or even my dad
The new friends I've made
Or the old friends I had?

My head's in a whirl
With no clear vision.

Thomas Kay (11)
Little Lever School (Specialist Language College)

My Poem

My poem is about a poem,
You know about the sky and sea.
The poem is about *the* poem,
The one I like.

My poem is about a poem,
You know about the sun and trees.
My poem is about *the* poem,
The one I like.

My poem is about a poem,
You know about the wind and breeze.
My poem is *the* poem,
The one I like.

My poem is my poem,
The one you've just read.

Kelly-Louise Graveson (12)
Little Lever School (Specialist Language College)

Hopeless Hag

(A Hallowe'en poem)

'That's rubbish! Get it right!'
It's the same routine every night,
I'm training to be a witch, to perform magic.
To show off in mid-air on my oaken broomstick.
Rabbits out of top hats, a weed into a rose
I only succeed in getting up my teacher's nose.
'Stupid child, you're hopeless!' they always cry.
I look down at myself, I guess they're right.

I can't do spells; they just go up in smoke,
My potions have become a family joke!
My broomstick's none other than a daft flying log!
I don't have a black cat. I've just got my dog.
To top it all off, my wand's just a toy!
All the other kids tease me, both the girls and the boys.

'You'll never be evil,' my teacher finally sobs.
'Just leave, don't bother, get a mortal job!'
I leave the room at a supersonic pace,
Praying they don't notice the smile on my face.

Woo hoo! Fantastic! I'm finally free!
No more rancid potions! No more spells for me!
I'm outta here! Bye-bye! I can do what I like.
Chuck my broom in the bin, 'cause I'm buying a bike!

Jennifer Mort (13)
Little Lever School (Specialist Language College)

A Year Of . . .

Every day is a different thing,
We never know what it can bring.
In the morning you can hear the little birds sing,
It's just a year of happiness.

December, January and February are
When snow and rain fall everywhere,
This is what the clouds do share,
Months of cold winter chills,
And the beautiful trees start going bare.

March, April and May are
When the flower buds start to grow,
And the bright coloured petals start to show,
All the trees show their bright lime leaves,
The cold and blustery winds know where to go!

June, July and August are
When families are out on the beach,
There is no time for people to teach,
Because fun is the only word around,
Sadness here, is very hard to reach.

September, October and November are
When the autumn leaves fall to the ground,
By small children conkers are found,
Wet and windy weather occurs,
And you can feel the wind blowing round and round.

Taiba Abbas (14)
Little Lever School (Specialist Language College)

Death Lives On

Death is the shadow that follows the old,
It lingers in graveyards and forms a fear.
In hospital beds where the spirits live on,
Death is the stain that won't go away.
It takes over like a disease through the vein,
Like a cancer taking hold.
Death is the god of the underworld.
He has no feeling or senses,
But he knows who is going to be next.
Invisible to the eye, but leaves a trace,
Of agony, mourning and grief.
Hell fires burn, but death is immortal.
People run, but cannot escape,
Death, like a blood clot in the brain.
A knife through the heart,
A bomb unseen.
Death is a hand that takes the life.
Stealing it and throwing it away without a second glance.
A normal day with normal people, what do they know?
They could be laughing, but unaware they are suffering.
Death is not an optimist, but a realist.
Nothing can stop it.
So where is Jesus now?

Helen Gildert (16)
Little Lever School (Specialist Language College)

My Brave Brother

My brother is so brave
He goes away to the army
I miss him a lot
Sometimes it makes me cry.

I've always known my brother was brave
Going like that
I look at his picture and remember him
My bigger brother who stuck up for me.

Nicola Ross (11)
Little Lever School (Specialist Language College)

Inexpressible Feelings

The writer paused,
Empty echoes resounding
Warnings of avoidance.
To delve amidst the
Depths of an
Endless emotion.

The writer untameable,
Coils of a ribbon,
Frayed along the perforations.
Yet within, reflecting
Pristine, silken innocence.

The writer disregarding,
Callous whispers of caution.
A journey, never to
Be suppressed.
A gulf, unimaginable
Breached.

As to the subject . . .
Reflected in a mother's gaze.
Captured in the morning dew.
Suspended comfort in familiar silence.
Meaningless clichés.

The writer blank
Inadequacy plagued the page.
To define the subject,
A word created
As the result of
Inexpressible feelings.

Kirsty Gilchrist (16)
Little Lever School (Specialist Language College)

When Snow Is Fun

When I look outside in the night,
Snow is falling everywhere,
From the floor to the sky,
The night looks quite white.

I love playing in the snow.
Slipping here and slipping there,
While people stand and stare.
Will she fall or will she slip,
Or will she just land on her hip?

Picking snowball fights with my brother,
Until he goes crying back to Mother,
'She's making me wet,' he wails,
It's not hard, it's really soft,
Just like my softy brother.

Making snowmen rolling with the snow,
Using carrots for his nose,
And big, fat buttons for his smile,
With a coat round his waist,
As though he is going to be a while.

As the sun comes out to play,
The snowman starts to melt away.
Into water he will turn,
Waiting for the time of his return.

Sabreena Bari
Little Lever School (Specialist Language College)

An Ode To A Nurse Who Helped Me Get Through It All

Thank you to you, nurse,
Who helped me,
And for being there,
Every day,

And helped me to see how lucky I am,
That I have good friends and family,
Who are always there for me,
To support me all the time.

You were there day and night,
Making sure I was alright,
Keeping me comfy,
All snuggled in my bed.

You held my hand when I was scared,
And helped me through my problem,
By making me laugh and smile all day,
So this is what I have to say . . .

'You are the best nurse in the world,
And you should get a prize,
Because you are so wonderful,
In every way there is.'

Thank you to the nurse,
Who helped me.

Erin Kirkman (15)
Little Lever School (Specialist Language College)

My Football Team

My football team,
We are all so keen,
I'm glad we don't play in the morning
Or else we would be yawning.

I play in defence,
Because I am built like a fence,
I am very loud
As there is never a crowd!

We try very hard
Not to get a red card,
We never seem to win,
We should get chucked in the bin!

Jason Critchley (11)
Little Lever School (Specialist Language College)

The Rain

The rain falls down silent
Not saying a word
Though you can hear it
It cannot be heard
It swoops down from the sky
From way, way up high
And glistens in the moonlight
Until the first breath of sunlight
Clears the dark sky.

Amy Louise Coward (11)
Little Lever School (Specialist Language College)

I Wish It Was Summer

The sun's rays peer around your curtains,
Opening them you have to squint.

It's warm outside already,
You walk along the street.

Children are running,
Playing happily.

The ice cream van comes into view
It'll already be melted,
Kids run up anyway.

Wish it was summer.

Emma Round (15)
Little Lever School (Specialist Language College)

The Fun Of The Fair

The fun of the fair for all to share,
Children giggling everywhere,
Fast rides, slow rides, big rides too.
There's always something for us to do.
Candyfloss, lots of sweets,
Children love their little treats.
Big wheel, waltzer, Haunted House
Makes me squeal like a little mouse.
Now it's time to leave the fair
We'll be back again next year.

Megan Lowe (12)
Little Lever School (Specialist Language College)

Love

Red is the colour of love.
Roses represent love.
Without love there would be hatred.

Luckily there is love everywhere.
Love lights up the world.
You never know when you have fallen in love.
Valentine's is a day for love.
Love is a relationship, a bond between two people.
Looks bring people together,
But personality brings them closer.

Zara Farukh (11)
Little Lever School (Specialist Language College)

Sweet Shop

Creamy caramel
Ice cream treats,
Milky Way bars!
Lots of sugared sweets.

Cool Coca-Cola drinks,
Sticky golden honey,
Candyfloss (a real treat),
And chocolate money!

Bethany Evenett (11)
Little Lever School (Specialist Language College)

My Poem

We are all human beings,
None of us the same,
We all like different things,
People call us by our name.

In all shapes and sizes,
Different in many ways,
We enjoy lots of fun
And hobbies that last for days.

So no one is the same,
This I am sure you knew,
As I said, we all are different
Like me and like you.

David Potts (11)
Little Lever School (Specialist Language College)

My Fun In The Sun

I love holidays in the sun,
I have so much fun.
I love to keep cool,
just floating in the pool.
I wear my shades,
whilst digging with my bucket and spade.
I have fun on the water slides,
and on the fair rides.
I lick my ice cream,
it is such a dream.
Oh, how I love the sun,
my fun in the sun.

Lucy Woodiwiss (13)
Little Lever School (Specialist Language College)

Hallowe'en

The ghostly ghouls of a scary night,
It's Hallowe'en so bring out the fright.
People knocking on the doors,
Children wanting treats and more.

Goblins, ghouls, monsters and creeps,
Rustling in the bushes about to leap.
The drooling werewolf looks up at the full moon,
He's getting hungry so there will be a victim soon.

Witches lurking in the shadow of the night,
Ready to give someone a fright,
The ghostly ghouls of a scary night,
It's Hallowe'en so bring out the fright.

Claire McGovern (11)
Little Lever School (Specialist Language College)

Pets

Let me tell you of my pets,
I assure you I've got many.
We are hardly ever at the vets
Because they all are healthy.

You'll want to know their names.
The dogs are Meg and Lucky.
The budgie's now called James.
My cat is really Bonny.

Danielle Whitley (11)
Little Lever School (Specialist Language College)

What I'd Do Without My Uncle

Without my uncle, life would be gloomy,
he is hip-hop and tip top!
The best uncle I know!

My uncle is funky, kind, fun and cool,
he shouts and screams and he stamps his feet
but he is still my number one uncle.

One day my uncle said he would
take me to Hollywood to be a star.
I said, 'I'm a star, here with you!'

Now my uncle is dying, I said,
'We will not be able to go now, but
I'll be a star thinking of you!'

And I know when my uncle dies
I'll see the bright star in the sky above
And that star will be my uncle,
Sending down to me his love.

Leah Kelly (12)
Our Lady's Catholic College

Autumn

Leaves all around me,
Lots of different colours,
Golden yellow, bronze, fiery red,
They fall from the trees to the ground,
All the children wrap up warm,
Screeching with excitement,
Crunching leaves under my feet,
It's too cold,
Snow starts to fall,
Night draws in,
Summer has gone.

Zoë Cannar (11)
Our Lady's Catholic College

Cats

Cats look fluffy
cats look cute
but they're not nice
they eat all your rice
they go through your milk
and sleep on your silk

Cats are silly
they hurt Uncle Billy
they bring in birds
and eat all your nerds
they bite your toes
and scratch your nose

Cats are scary
and very hairy
they put on your shoes
and drink all your booze

So if you want a cat
and your name is Pat
just think about this carefully
because cats are mean
and they're not clean.

Hannah Webster (11)
Our Lady's Catholic College

My Nephew Is . . .

My nephew's younger than your nephew
yes, my nephew's younger than yours
he was only born on the 6th of May
yes, my nephew roars and snores.

My nephew plays longer than your nephew
yes, my nephew plays longer than yours
he likes to play with cars all night
when he plays with cars, he roars

My nephew eats more than your nephew
yes, my nephew eats more than yours
he loves to eat bics and crisps, that's a fact
well he eats, then snores and snores.

My nephew's cuter than your nephew
yes, my nephew's cuter than yours
he has a cute, smiley face with little rosy cheeks
well he's cute, even when he snores.

Leah Bradford (11)
Our Lady's Catholic College

1st Prize Draw

This is what I set out to do,
To write this poem to impress you.

I really hope it'll do the job,
If it doesn't, I'll try not to sob.

For the whole lesson I was writing this,
The first prize, I hope not to miss.

I really don't know what to say,
Thinking of rhyme turns my mind to clay.

I need to finish for it is due,
I really hope this has impressed you!

Peter Townsend (11)
Our Lady's Catholic College

Dancing

I go to Happy Feet
That's a dancing school
We dance to a beat,
It is really, really cool

Sarah is our teacher
She's very, very kind
In a show we feature
Dancing in a line

I really enjoy it
It's cool to dance
It keeps you really fit
When you prance.

Abigail Gray (11)
Our Lady's Catholic College

Candyfloss

C andyfloss
A pple pie
N ougat
D oughnuts
Y oghurt
F ish pie
L ots of food
O ld and new
S ugar and
S weets

All the yummy things I like to eat,
Apart from the fish pie, which tastes of a . . . fish eye!

Megan McCallum (11)
Our Lady's Catholic College

The Darkness Of Night

The darkness of the night
Is a monster's delight,
Where ghouls and ghosts go out to fright.
Kids look under their beds in dread.
But the ghosts are hiding in the wardrobe instead.
The monsters come out and grab the kids tight
And the kids shiver in fright.
But soon morning comes and they're back in bed.
I wonder if they realise they're dead . . . ?
The ghosts are hiding underground,
Making nothing of a sound . . . waiting and waiting
Until they're hunted down . . .

Lucy Tomlinson (12)
Our Lady's Catholic College

Is There Anybody There?

It's cold and eerie, I wonder if I'm alone,
I can hear the rain thunder on the outside world.

There's someone here different to me,
Will I find it or will it find me?
I think it's a bat; red eyes glowing,
Or maybe a glow-worm hovering in the
Midnight air.

There's a voice inside me
That tells me to run,
But should I run or should I stay?
My forehead is sweating,
What is this creature in front of me?

Rachel Bates (11)
Ripley St Thomas CE High School

The Elephant Song

The baby elephant cries in disbelief,
His mother killed by an ivory thief.

His eyes began to fill with tears,
As the hunters ran with their spears.

He snuggles beside her silent heart,
Where it all started with just one dart.

His mother's ears as soft as leather,
That once protected her from the weather.

The baby elephant cries in disbelief,
His mother killed by an ivory thief.

Here he is now in the sanctuary pen,
Fortunately, the world is not full of bad men.

He will miss his mother for evermore,
So please, please stand by this animal law.

The baby elephant cries in disbelief,
His mother killed by an ivory thief.

So think of the elephants where they
Should roam.

Instead of ivory trinkets found in
Your home.

Loren Kyles-Ashton (11)
Ripley St Thomas CE High School

Winter

W inter is here, Jack Frost is about,
 I n the caves are sharp icicles like eagle claws coming out,
N ear a cliff, it swoops down like a burning fire,
T rees are bare like broken bones,
E very tree is beaten, broken and brown, with the
                                            tornadoes of leaves,
R ed robins flutter down like rainfall falling on the ground.

Sophie Wilson (11)
Ripley St Thomas CE High School

The Final!

Rugby is a game of skill,
Rugby is a test of will,
You'll go far built like iron,
But even further with the heart of a lion.

Rugby ball spinning around,
Rugby ball on the ground,
It's a race to the ball,
First team there wins the maul.

The ball is won,
The score is tight,
The tension's up,
We've got to fight.

The fly half has it,
A minute to go,
Kicks for glory,
A final blow.

The flags are raised,
The trophy's near,
What a game,
We deserved the cheer!

Oliver McNamara (14)
Ripley St Thomas CE High School

Mrs May Thinks I'm Reading But I'm . . .

Mrs May thinks I'm reading but I'm . . .
Swimming around a desert island,
Skating on the Arctic Ocean,
Flying high with the birds,
Space walking on Mars,
Mrs May thinks I'm reading and I am!

Emily Stocks (11)
Ripley St Thomas CE High School

Feeling

If love is patient, then love is blind.
If love is forgiveness, then love is kind.
Love can shine like a thousand stars and
Be as vast as the deepest oceans.
It can be like a flower that blossoms,
Into the midnight sun or it can wither,
Die or fade into the night.
Love could be a first kiss or
Love can make millions of people cry with
Joy and happiness or it can make tears
Of unimaginable pain,
Like weeping for a lost soul.
But when you see that right person and
Gaze into glistening eyes then true love
Can unfold right in front of you,
That is the greatest feeling
Anyone can feel!

Faye Cameron (13)
Ripley St Thomas CE High School

Boy Warrior

I put on my helmet
Slash watering can,
And think up a name,
Like Battle Ready Dan.

I pull out my sword,
Well perhaps it's a stick,
I thrust it forward,
At my friend Nick.

We hack and we slash,
Until our stomachs do rumble,
And inside of my house,
Waits a warrior's crumble.

William Hunt (11)
Ripley St Thomas CE High School

My Family

In all the years I've lived at home,
I've never been left on my own,
But the day I started at high school you see,
My mum and dad gave me a key.

'When you come home, you'll be the first one in,'
Said my mum, with a big, wide grin,
But when the clocks changed and I let myself in,
It was cold, it was dark and I bumped into the bin.

I switched on the lights and made for my room,
And started my homework, it's as cold as a tomb,
Then there's a click and the heat comes on,
So I go to the kitchen and put the tea on.

My family arrive home and ask about my day,
My mum and dad take over and do things their way,
I don't mind helping, we're a family you see,
My mum, my dad, my brother and me.

Olivia Jamin (12)
Ripley St Thomas CE High School

A Secret You May Not Know About Teachers!

Teachers aren't real,
They're not like you or me,
Teachers are made from text book knowledge,
Then given away for free!

They're packed into big cardboard boxes,
With a coffee mug at the back,
With a packet of marking pens,
And a 'how to be a teacher' pack!

After they've been unpacked,
They'll have a big school tour,
They practice giving detentions,
Then they come through someone's classroom door!

Charlotte Brown (12)
Ripley St Thomas CE High School

The Song Of The Elephant

Elephant with your snake-like trunk,
In the water you bathe and dunk,
Your dagger-like tusks stand out so clear,
And you always know when terror is near,
Your ears are used to keep you cool,
Hunters that kill you are so cruel.

Oh elephant in your different ways,
We hope you see some happy days.

Elephant in your colourful suit,
Looking intelligent yet still cute,
They dress you in make-up, oh poor thing,
And you have to listen to performers sing,
You do gymnastics and tightrope too,
The audience just loves watching you.

Oh elephant in your different ways,
We hope you see some happy days.

Elephant in that dreadful zoo,
Visitors come to look at you,
They tie you to a cold damp chain,
And leave you to suffer in dreadful pain,
They feed you half of what you need,
In your cage you beg to be freed.

Oh elephant in your different ways,
We hope you see some happy days.

Hannah Jackson (11)
Ripley St Thomas CE High School

A Warning To Parents

There once was a boy called Owen John Dunne
Whose parents prevented him from having any fun
They locked him in his bedroom
They took away his toys,
They stood him in the garden
And forbade him to make noise
And as I'm sure you will have thought,
The disasters to the lad it brought,
He spent the day uttering curses,
And even stole old ladies' purses!
But worst of all this awful boy
Had thought of the most dreadful ploy
To assassinate the Queen of Britain
And then to steal her little kitten!
The evil boy crept to the palace,
And with thoughts just full of malice,
Crept up past the Queen's best Corgi
(Which answered to the name of Porgy)
He hit the Queen upon the head
And grabbed the kitten from her bed
But this kitten was a ferocious beast
Not cute or cuddly in the least,
It tore the evil boy to shreds
And then proceeded to eat his head.

Moral -   Oh parents dear
          Whatever you do
          Be kind to each other
          But also sons too!

Owen Dunne (11)
Ripley St Thomas CE High School

Stuck In A Lift

Lift doors open
I glide inside
Preparing for a
Smooth swift ride.

It's rather packed
There's not much air
I find the temperature
Hard to bear.

Crammed with people
Some tall
Some short
Babies crying
Parents fraught.

Doors open wide
At level three
Everyone exits
Except for me.

I press the button
For one level more
I'm all alone
I feel unsure.

It's slow to move
Panic rises
I don't want any
Nasty surprises.

My heart beats faster
I'm very stressed
It creaks and groans
I'm not impressed!

Shudders and jerks
A sudden jolt
Deathly *silence*!
Grinds to a halt.

A sudden drone
The lights go out
I'm stuck in a lift
There's no way out!

Kate Corfield (12)
Ripley St Thomas CE High School

Please . . .

I lay awake, I cannot sleep,
For in the night I begin to weep,
I think about the next day,
And wonder when I can finally play,
. . . Please, care for me.

The day begins, I hear you shout,
And hit the room and me about,
Because I made you mad again,
I don't mean to cause you pain,
. . . Please, forgive me.

It's sunset now, I sit in fear,
I know I made you depressed all year,
I know you wish you never had me,
Then you'd have never been a daddy,
. . . Please, understand me.

I lay there, I cannot breath,
There is silence now, I cannot hear you shout,
There's no more fear, I cannot feel any pain,
. . . It's over
. . . I was born to die.

Heather Cross (14)
Ripley St Thomas CE High School

Terrorist Attack

All was happy and normal that day,
The sun came up and then went away,
Each child was working in the school that day,
All happy, joyful and eager to play.

Families were together at the start of that day,
Terrorists came and took that away,
Everyone was shocked and full of dismay.

The world in shock, there was no more play,
We held our breath for too long that day.

That day in Russia was a sad, sad day,
All had been well in the school that day,
Until the sadness came and didn't go away,
The shots were heard, the terror would stay,
In all our hearts and not go away.

We will remember those children that died that day,
Bodies have gone but the memories will stay.

Peter Kneale (13)
Ripley St Thomas CE High School

Boys!

Some boys' brains are made of jelly,
Some of them are really smelly!
Some boys are funny and quite cool,
Some of them really rule!

Some boys are stupid and very thick,
Most of them need a right good kick!
Some of them are nice to me,
Though only one, two or maybe three!

Some boys love to have a laugh,
Some of them need to have a bath!
Most of them are a waste of time,
And this is why I wrote this rhyme!

Stephanie Wood (11)
Ripley St Thomas CE High School

Pies

I despise pies.
With all the fuss,
It causes for us.
The prices,
And spices.
Decisions,
Revisions.
Which pastry,
Is most tasty?
Should it be sweet,
Or savoury with meat?
Many a flavour,
To savour.
But as it grows old,
It grows mould.
Or leaves a fuzz.
A pie does.

Simon Saunders (11)
Ripley St Thomas CE High School

The Lakes

For the beauty of our bonny county,
We'll welcome you all with a smile,
And you will enjoy every mile of its beauty
From Kendal right up to Carlisle,
And down that great Eden valley,
Where the Eden sweeps down to the sea,
Cross fell looks out with all his glory,
Way out to the wild Irish Sea,
To the west, there's the Cumbrain Mountains,
Their beauty no tongue can describe,
For there's Scafell, Helvelyne and Saddle Back,
And a whole host of others beside.

Andrew Drummond (12)
Ripley St Thomas CE High School

Why Are Children Involved?

Why are children involved?
Why are they involved in wars and conflict?
What have they done to deserve their families killed
Brutally in front of their young eyes?
Why should that make them scared and think the world is like that?

Why should children be beaten when they do wrong,
Or if they haven't done anything at all?
Do people want to show them that violence is the only good
Thing in life, and that is better than a parent's love?
Why should they have disease and viruses or be diagnosed
With disabilities as soon as they enter this world,
Even though they are innocent?

If children ruled the world, there would be no war,
No hatred or anger. It would be a safe place to live
As there would be no murderers or criminals in the world.
The world would be a place of peace and harmony with
No fear of danger and wars.

So, why should children be involved?

Oliver David Bray (15)
Ripley St Thomas CE High School

Pleated Bows

Bows, pleated with human hands,
Scented, with herbs from all around,
Celery, plums, wheat and grain,
Farmers, working through the pain.

Entering the great decorative church hall,
We lay our gifts on the floor,
The vicar worships our harvest gifts,
Now we take them all around,
To houses for people to enjoy and be proud,
These bows pleated by human hands,
Scented, with herbs from all around.

Hannah Jackson & Loren Kyles-Ashton (11)
Ripley St Thomas CE High School

A Poem For Christmas

As
I look
Out of the
Window,
I wish it could snow,
Though all it is, is rain, rain, rain,
Oh how it,
Is such a pain,
Children are counting down,
Until St Nicholas comes to town,
All the shops are really busy,
Shoppers rush round and make you dizzy.
People are panicking, they haven't bought enough,
From Christmas presents,
To delicious plum duff!
It's Christmas Eve and no one can sleep,
So I creep downstairs to have a peep,
At all the presents tucked under the tree,
I wonder excitedly, *which ones are for me?*
The best part of Christmas has yet to come,
I creep back up to bed and dream of all the fun!

Emily Inston (13)
Ripley St Thomas CE High School

Untitled

Throwing
On the tinsel
As the tree goes up.
Baubles going everywhere
As I look up. As I look up I see the
Shiny star glistening in the moonlight.
I stop and I think what Christmas is all about,
Is it the presents or the loving and the caring?

James Birchall (14)
Ripley St Thomas CE High School

Two Minutes Silence

Oh God! What do we have to remember?
'Remember, remember the fifth of November.'
Gunpowder plots, sparklers and fires,
Guy Fawkes, firework explosions and . . .
But that was last week.

What's Tom doing? What's he starring at?
Could it be that spot on slimy Sam's nose?
I wonder what's for lunch,
Ham sandwich, chocolate cake and apple juice,
Oh I wish I could have a McDonald's instead,
I'm starrvvviiiinnnggg . . . starving.

What's Lucy doing? Why's she inspecting her nails?
Is she allowed to paint them bright red?
They look like blooming claws,
Oh no disgusting Den is picking his nose,
My God! His whole finger has got lost up there,
Mustn't laugh . . . mustn't laugh . . .

How much longer? I want to go!
Look at my shoes, I should have polished them,
Wish I'd revised my French last night,
Shouldn't have been watching Little Britain!
I wonder if Tom'll lend me 'Hogs of War,'
Ooh at last . . . at last.

I should care even if I wasn't involved and I wasn't there,
They gave their lives, their health and limbs,
They gave themselves, brothers, husbands and sons,
They gave their today's for our tomorrow's,
I couldn't even give them two minutes,
So ashamed . . . ashamed . . .

Ricky Cusimano (11)
Ripley St Thomas CE High School

The Trial

No judge or jury gathered here,
To decide her fate,
No Bible to give oath on,
No lawyers to debate.

Her eyes watered with the fire,
Her heart was her own drum,
Beating with the dread,
Of knowing what's to come,
She reached into the heat,
And grasped the glowing rod,
Her searing flesh and blistering pain,
A step at the priest's nod,
Each pace seemed an eternity,
As it burnt into her palm,
Struggling to fight the urge to scream,
Trying to stay calm,
Eight paces left and her arm shot pain,
Burning up into her soul,
Her agony fought against her mind,
Her heart a gaping hole,
Too much pain to bear inside,
Wrestling to be freed,
Her throat was gagging to cry aloud,
An overwhelming need,
One last step to end the trial,
Her hand snapping free,
The iron bar tumbles down,
She's changed her destiny,
All that's left is now a memory,
Written by the brand,
Embedded deep into her skin,
Scored across her hand.

Emily Casey (13)
Ripley St Thomas CE High School

The Elephant

The elephant, huge and mighty,
Its murky grey skin covers a great,
Heavy, colossal body.

A long, unique, flexible trunk
Curves to drink steadily,
Tree trunk-like legs move it slowly,
Dawdling and thumping heavily,
Its large white ears cool it from the African sun.

This creature's strong, snow-white tusks,
Rip off lush green leaves and tree bark,
Which it consumes with great appetite and hunger.

This magnificent mammal when the sun goes down,
Rests on the golden plains of Africa.

Rachel Roberts (11)
Ripley St Thomas CE High School

The Day

I woke up this morning and it
Was sunny outside,
But when I remembered the day,
I could've cried!
The start of the school year,
Oh no! I can hear my mum's
Footsteps coming near.

'Wake up darling, get out of bed!
And put on your school head!'

Help! It's time for school!
Ah, I'll use my famous tool.

'Ow! My tummy, my tummy!
I can't go to school today Mummy!'

Farrah Boutros (11)
Ripley St Thomas CE High School

My Jungle

You can't see my jungle, crowded with fresh,
Emerald leaves.
My hamster can't either, who is buried in her bed.

My jungle is far, far away, in a completely unique world.

There are no broken bones and no hurt elbows,
But if you're not careful, strange animals may be
Lurking in the shadows.

Also, there are flowers, red, orange, yellow, blue, purple and
Pink, as bright as the sun.
They cover my jungle like a flock of sheep,
Crowded in a certain area.

You can even ride on elephants,
Chase jaguars and sleep with the cheeky monkeys.

All of a sudden, the apples play the drums and
The rattlesnakes rattle.

But the best thing is, you can't see my jungle,
And neither can my hamster,
Who is still buried in her bed.

Rosanna Wood (11)
Ripley St Thomas CE High School

War

War is not pretty,
War is not fun,
Some people think it still should be done,
War is like Hell,
Red with blood,
Surely we would stop it if we only could,
War is not happy,
Loved ones are lost,
You may win the battle, but at what cost?

Joe Higginson (12)
Ripley St Thomas CE High School

Poem For The Children Of The World

Isn't home where the heart is?
Isn't home supposed to be a place of love?

For the lucky ones yes, yes it is,
But for the increasing number no, no it isn't.

Many children now,
Are affected by rows.

Rows between parents,
Or rows between a parent and them?

Some violence may break out
Children too scared to speak about.

They may be beaten,
Thinking they might be eaten.

We need to help
We need to help out.

Jessica Stainer (14)
Ripley St Thomas CE High School

I Should Like To . . .

I should like to touch the dazzling colours of the rainbow,
I should like to touch the shaggy mane of a unicorn,
I should like to see a rabbit flying, soaring through the clouds,
Or the wind rushing through the trees,
I should like to hear the animals, big and small,
Chatting wildly to each other,
I should like to hear a song that nobody is singing,
I should like to smell the fresh paint of Titanic,
And the smell of music,
I should like to taste the pages of my favourite novel.

Emma Brzezinka (11)
Ripley St Thomas CE High School

Words Never Spoken . . .

Those long nights of bliss and pleasure,
Stay in my mind like golden treasure,
Your hands and mine joined together,
Entwined and protecting in eternity forever.

Those words were never spoken,
Those words I needed to hear,
Until that dreaded night of pain,
The death that you and I fear.

When all was right and you were here,
And the path of friendship was plain and clear,
You had your chance to tell me your feelings,
Until that night that sent me reeling.

Those words were never spoken,
Those words I needed to hear,
Until that dreaded night of pain,
The death that you and I fear.

Sometimes I sit and cry all night,
I wonder if you can see this sight,
Not the jolly person of the past,
Just a weeping wreck, that's out of your grasp.

Those words were never spoken,
Those words I needed to hear,
Until that dreaded night of pain,
The death that you and I fear.

People can laugh and joke at me,
But to that treasure I'll hold the key,
And even though you're not here,
To tackle with me that hate and fear,
I'll make it through hard times and new,
Knowing the fact you never said, 'I love you.'

Emma Gardner (14)
Ripley St Thomas CE High School

9/11

American, British the list never ends,
The culprits we'll find, you can depend,
All of those people, what had they done?
They were making a living and had hurt no one,
The USA now has to cope with the pain,
We hope it's all over and won't happen again.

It has been three years now since that terrible day,
When New York's skyline was changed in that way,
The World Trade Centre is not there anymore,
The visions reappear when it collapsed to the floor,
Thousands of innocent people had lost their lives,
Some of them fathers, mothers and wives.

Each passing day we think of those who died,
Airport security increased worldwide,
Never again must the world suffer this loss,
The terrorists will learn they can never be boss!
All we can do is learn from that fateful day,
Think of those families torn apart and *pray!*

Josh Smith (13)
Ripley St Thomas CE High School

Courage

Courage does not have to be a thing of knights and steeds,
Or a tale of dreams like slaying giant millipedes,
It could be something as trivial as facing your smallest fears,
Or standing up to bullies both big and strong,
Courage is doing right when everyone else is doing wrong,
So put down your daggers, put down your swords,
Lower your shields and stand up tall,
For courage does not come from strength,
But from deep down in your soul.

Ross Jesmont (13)
Ripley St Thomas CE High School

Bonfire Night

It was all silent, all still and all dark,
Cats roamed the streets with no worries in the world,
Then suddenly a light filled the sky like a rainbow exploding,
Another and another all different but not one the same.

Adults start clapping at the sight,
Little children started crying in fright,
It stood roaring like a lion trapped in a cage.

The light stopped filling up the sky,
The little children stopped crying,
The adults stopped clapping,
And the lion stopped roaring.

And it was all silent again,
All still and dark,
And cats roamed the streets again
With no worries in the world.

Lizzy Wilkinson (13)
Ripley St Thomas CE High School

These I Have Loved!

The sight and feel of the crisp new fallen snow,
The taste of freshly baked bread with layers of real butter,
The sight of new spring-bloomed snowdrops,
The feel and sound of my horse neighing as I wake in the morning,
To see a blue, bright clear sky with a big rainbow arched through it,
To also hear the birds singing as I wake in the morning,
The sight of the sun setting behind the mountain, leaving
A painted colour through it.
The feel of baby soft skin,
The taste of a scone with jam, butter and cream on,
The smell of a freshly baked apple pie, just come out of the oven,
To see the newborn lambs in springtime bound around like springs,
The feel of a freshly made bed, as you snuggle down to
                    sleep at night, beneath the starry sky.

Emily Greenhalgh (13)
Ripley St Thomas CE High School

A Dog Is A Dog

Mongrel or pedigree,
Robust or frail,
He still has a mind,
Four legs and a tail.

Just like us
He deserves a life,
Free from cruelty,
Hardship and strife.

Through thick and thin,
His master he serves,
Yet he rarely gets
The respect he deserves.

A dog doesn't understand,
The bitter blow from a cruel hand
He's not a thing to be abused,
A dog ill-treated is a dog confused.

Dogs are abandoned,
Without hesitation,
This is Britain, once renowned,
As a dog-loving nation.

This is our country,
In all its entirety,
Tell me what happened
To our caring society?

Rebecca Marwood (14)
Ripley St Thomas CE High School

The 10 Ages Of Women

At first we are a baby,
All we do is eat, sleep, cry,
And maybe gurgle on a good day,
Next we become a toddler,
Only just walking and very cheeky,
But we are quick to tire,
Then, a shy little schoolgirl,
Skipping happily along,
For her first lesson of the day,
This little girl transforms into a teenager,
Gossiping about the latest fashion,
Spending most of her time with her boyfriend,
Next a student,
Moved away from home and at university,
Where every day is a permanent hangover,
And a struggle for cash,
Then, the mother who juggles various part-time jobs,
With panda eyes from sleepless nights,
Free relief is on its way,
As we retire from our hectic job-ridden lives,
Every day is a rest, every month is a holiday!
The pensioner hobbles along carrying her crumbled bag
Reading *Oxfam* in large letters,
Regular trips to the bingo hall,
A night to look forward to,
Finally, old age takes over and death slips into place,
As we fall asleep peacefully in our favourite chair next to
The TV, never to wake.

Emma Barton (13)
Ripley St Thomas CE High School

These I Have Loved!

These I have loved:
The pot faces of the elves in Lord of the Rings,
Sunset, sunrise, the rings of flame and power,
The spray on your face in the shower, like it releases you,
Leaves swaying and falling until they hit the ground, the quiet thud,
Squirts of juice from a Braeburn apple,
Howard Castle when the frost smothers its windows and grounds,
Closing my eyes, visions I see of what I want to be,
The dreams I have weird and wacky,
I love the touch of cats when they sweep past you unnoticed,
Reading books and getting magical visions, of untrue worlds,
The beat of rock music running through your open ears,
Tears falling like raindrops, onto an unexpecting surface,
To sketch a face in detail to make it come alive,
I hear trickling water over river stones,
Scenic countryside silent as gold,
The smell of shortbread cooking in the oven, the anticipation,
I love to laugh so the pressures of the world disappear,
Opening curtains not expecting snow, but there it is a
Layer of pure white.

Amy Westworth (13)
Ripley St Thomas CE High School

One Snowy Morning

The blanket of snow twinkles in the sunlight,
The only sound was snow falling gracefully on the ground,
Snowflakes look so silky they keep falling, falling down,
The canal is frozen and glistens like a twinkling star.

Charlotte Philipson (13)
Ripley St Thomas CE High School

These I Have Loved

These I have loved:
The sight of the shining moon at night,
The sound of an owl taking off in flight,
A rainbow's colours, the grassy smell,
My terrapin as it goes into its shell,
A crackling fire when it's freezing cold,
The sun on my face making me stand out bold,
The taste of chocolate as it melts down my throat,
Looking down at the water from a luxury boat,
The taste of strawberries all juicy red,
The look of a forest in which leaves have been shed,
The feel of sand between my feet,
A comfortable bed with a brand new sheet,
The gorgeous smell of fish and chips,
Playing my Xbox as I flick through the tips,
The trickling water from a nearby stream,
The light of the day as I wake from a dream,
The feel of a feather soft on my cheek,
The joy of my bed at the end of the week,
The sight of a tree standing tall,
These I have loved, these I've loved all.

Lewis Cockerill (13)
Ripley St Thomas CE High School

Flying Cakes From Outer Space

Cakes, cakes from outer space,
They're flying around all over the place,
Cakes from Venus,
Cakes from Mars,
They have cream from Jupiter,
And jam from the stars.
They whiz around and over trees,
When they're carried around in the breeze.

Christina Wren (13)
Ripley St Thomas CE High School

God's Creation

The first thing that God made,
Was of course light,
Followed on by darkness
As well as day and night.

The second thing that God made,
Was the pale blue sky,
To store His home, to share with souls,
And the difference of low and high.

The third thing that God made,
Was the sea and land,
The clear, fresh sea water,
Bordered by silky white sand.

The next things that God made,
Belong in the sky,
It's the sun, moon and stars,
Oh! So way up high.

The fifth and sixth things that God made,
Were animals and plants,
From roses to lions to eagles,
And spiders to creepy ants.

The last thing that God made
Was of course the man
To save His world from evil
And protect His brand new land.

As God's work was over
And all work was done
God deserved a well-earned rest
As His creation started and begun.

Jane Salisbury (13)
Ripley St Thomas CE High School

These I Have Loved

These I have loved:

Watching the world through my television,
The mesmerising look of the tranquil stream,
A distant rainbow shining in the sunny sky,
And the graceful eagle flying by.

Playing as a team in football, rugby or cricket,
Competing on my own in a race and trying to win it.
The smell of chocolate cake baking in the oven,
The whistle of the wind while I'm in a warm bed,
The warming feel of a cat's fur,
The taste of chocolate melting on my tongue.

Going on holiday and playing in the sun,
Swimming in a swimming pool and having great fun,
Playing a tune on my clarinet and making a sound I like,
Riding around far and wide on a mountain bike.

Sleeping in my bed to recover from a hard day,
Reading a good book and being transported to a world far away,
Having lots of fun playing on my games console,
FIFA 2004 is my favourite game after scoring a good goal.

The sound of the school bell on Friday at the end of the day,
Monday morning seems far, far away.

Rupert Callingham (13)
Ripley St Thomas CE High School

Poem

There was a man from Corfu,
Who had trouble flushing the loo,
The handle was stuck,
He was out of luck,
And didn't know what to do.

Peter Smyth (13)
Ripley St Thomas CE High School

Home Time

Most children are happy on the playground,
Games to play, bullies to defeat,
After school they go off happily to their homes
And see mummies' and daddies' happy smiling faces.

Whitney doesn't want to leave that playground though,
Surely the bully's better than Mummy and Daddy arguing about her,
The feel of a hand across her cheek for no reason,
Or the occasional beating that she didn't deserve?
What did she do to deserve this?

Later on it seems there is nowhere left to run or hide,
Wherever she goes they're going to find her,
Bloody and bruised she runs towards the door,
Maybe Louisa can help her,
But Daddy stands in the way,
What did she do to deserve this?

In one swift movement she's down on the cold, stone floor,
Falling lower and lower into the darkness,
Her breathing becomes shallow,
And then she sees it,
A light! The light that pierces the darkness.

She walks into it,
Happiness at last.

Jemma Smith (14)
Ripley St Thomas CE High School

Friends

Maybe it's cos I'm white,
Or maybe cos I'm black,
Everywhere we go, people stare and laugh.

We are best friends,
What is the problem?
We'll always stick together,
Best mates forever!

Alexandra Bolsover (13)
Ripley St Thomas CE High School

Winter

Icy mornings and slippery roads,
Fatal accidents with heavy loads,
Iced-up cars choking out white smoke,
Winter is coming with its white snowy cloak.

Snowy white snowmen looking wise,
The shiny black coal as their glistening eyes,
Chequered scarves and woolly hats,
To protect him from the snow as it pitter-pat-pats.

Gentle snowflakes tightly bound,
To form a white carpet on the ground,
Children sledging having fun,
Snowball fights played three to one.

The snow melts away, the fun is gone,
It's time for the snow clouds to move on,
The blue skies appear, the birds start to sing,
Winter has gone now to make way for *spring!*

Jenna Holden (13)
Ripley St Thomas CE High School

The Great Lover

These I have loved:
The crunch of the white snow under your feet,
The whoosh of air whizzing past your face,
Drive along in an open top car,
The beautiful sight of the sunset falling
Behind the snow-topped mountains,
The warmth of a cosy fire
Spreading over your face,
And the soft familiar voices of your family,
The pitter-patter of rain as it bounces off your windows,
The smell of melting butter as it fills your nasal,
The softness of my hamsters as they scatter over my hands.

Emily Dow (13)
Ripley St Thomas CE High School

The Dying Room

They look at me,
And I know what the look means,
I'm next,
I am going to the room.

This is the look everyone is dreading,
Fearing that they are going to be next,
But they have a few more days to worry,
Because I'm next.

I savour my last few moments,
Knowing that I will never see this room again,
Even if it does smell of death and illness,
I have lived here all my life,
I have had to wait with this fear,
Wondering who's next?

I have become numb to the pain,
The hatred and spitefulness,
That I have had to endure,
I try to block out the knowledge,
That everyone is waiting for me to die.

But still there is one thing I crave for,
Love.
The love that a mother and father give to their child,
The security that love brings,
And the joy of receiving it,
That is all I want,
But no one ever thought to say,
To an abandoned child,
'I love you.'

All I have had is my dungeon,
My cell that I live in.
The hard, cold and wetness,
Slices through my body every time I move,
My young heart has hardened to life,
But my will to live has died.

When you have done nothing wrong,
Except be born a girl,
Death is the worst punishment in life.

Faith Donaldson (14)
Ripley St Thomas CE High School

The Things That I Have Loved:

These I have loved:
The feeling of the cold crisp pillow,
The taste of garlic bread,
The smell of Lucozade orange,
The feeling of a hot mug
The taste of hot blackcurrant on a cold winter's day,
The feel of cold lemonade on a warm sunny day,
The clean crisp bedding,
The smell of a summer morn,
The freshness of a shower,
The smell of chips frying in a pan,
The comfort of my dog,
The softness of a couch,
The feel of the cricket ball thudding on my bat,
The smell in a bakery,
The water going up my nose,
As I jump into a pool,
Flying through the air,
As I tackle in despair,
The feel of the sand between my toes,
And a swim in a cold rock pool.

Stephen Tagg (13)
Ripley St Thomas CE High School

When The Lights Go Out

When the lights go out I'm blinded,
I'm deafened by the silence.
The thick heavy blanket of darkness takes my breath away,
I start to panic,
My eyes search the room for familiar objects,
Silhouettes make my eyes chase around the room,
I can feel myself becoming breathless,
I shut my eyes without a thought and hide underneath the covers,
I can't bear the tension of the atmosphere,
I begin to get hot and sticky,
But I can't put out my leg or arm, in case the thing
Under the bed grabs me!
A shadow lurks behind the curtains,
I'm not sure if it's moving,
It's moved behind my door,
Spiders crawl all over my bedspread,
The outside light eventually flickers on casting a welcoming
Glow into my room,
Then I realise there is no shadow in my window,
Only a dressing gown can be seen behind the door,
And the pretty daisies on my pink bedspread,
Appear not to have eight legs!

Lucy Stevenson (13)
Ripley St Thomas CE High School

Children Of The World

This is a poem for the children of the world,
Of which some may be homeless, starving or cold,
When others who are happy and safe in a house,
With three meals a day and a family who'll stay,
'They' don't know what it's like to have nothing,
To be a 'nothing'.
They are wanted, and they are loved!

Jane Harrison (14)
Ripley St Thomas CE High School

The Baby

Aunty Anne has had a baby
She brought her to the farm;
All warm and snuggled in a shawl
And wrapped in Auntie's arm.
When the baby woke, she cried,
Arms thrashing everywhere.
Until we showed the cows to her,
This made her stop and stare.

Then Mother held her gently,
And swayed her to and fro,
Baby smiled, sighed, then slept.
Until it was time to go,
Mother's face dropped and looked sad,
When the baby left her knee,
So I gave her dress a tug
And said,
'You still have Jack and me.'

Victoria Peill (14)
Ripley St Thomas CE High School

The World Through A Child's Eye

When I look at the world today,
I see so much hatred in the way,
Of life that could be so amazing,
With children playing, animals grazing,
And every now and then the snow falling on the ground.

With peace, happiness and love all around,
Instead each morning when I wake,
I'm greeted with war and no peace will they make,
My life's full of anger, hatred and rage,
Will there ever be peace in our day and age?

Lucy Hobbs (14)
Ripley St Thomas CE High School

Spring

Spring is here,
Summer is near,
Life's started again,
No worries, no pain.

She's like blossom on the tree,
Such a sight to see,
Her eyes are like sapphires,
Bet she's never seen the fires,
Her mouth whispers new life,
She hasn't heard of a knife,
And she will always be gentle,
So please don't call her mental,
As she is the one,
Who brings happiness and fun,
To plants, animals and Earth,
Her tears fall with mirth,
But they fall to the ground,
With no such sound,
Only to water everything,
And give new life with a meaning.

Spring is here,
Summer is near,
Life's started again,
No worries, no pain.

Heather Park (14)
Ripley St Thomas CE High School

Children Of The World

Children of the world
Different ages
Some treated like beasts in cages
Suffering silently
No one should be treated violently
Girls and boys
Some play with toys
Others cry
But we don't know why
They need our care
Because their parents aren't there
They don't know love
They have never seen the blue sky up above
Tortured and tied up
That's what's up
With the way they are treated
Abandoned and beaten
They have done nothing wrong
Maybe never spoken or sung a song
They are left to die
They are left to cry
Just show them that you care
By being there
They will be very pleased
Instead of being tortured and teased.

Matthew Liu (14)
Ripley St Thomas CE High School

Looking Down

Wrapped up in little bundles,
Half starved of real clothes to wear,
Looking down I can't help but wonder,
Of the evil who left them there.

Crying and screaming,
Tears of hurt and despair,
Looking down I can't help but wonder,
How a parent could leave their child there.

Deformed legs and puffed out eyes,
I can't help myself but stare,
Looking down I can't help but wonder,
How anyone could leave a baby there.

Hungry babies - deprived of food,
With no one to love or to care,
Looking down I can't help but wonder,
How any child could keep living there.

Children, tortured and tormented,
One hides behind a stair,
Then I look up to the sky and ask,
How can a child learn to love there?

Lucy Gager (14)
Ripley St Thomas CE High School

Chinese Orphanages

C loth is what they are wrapped in,
H ated and put in a bin,
I llness within them all,
L iving, until they fall,
D ying as we speak,
R ound about 1,000 a week,
E ngland is such a peaceful place,
N ever in China would you see a happy face.

Josh Atkinson (14)
Ripley St Thomas CE High School

To Children In Africa

I know your land called Africa,
I lived there for 10 years,
It's a land that has such beauty,
But its people have shed tears,
I know that life can seem so hard,
That no one really cares,
But we are thinking of you,
And will keep you in our prayers.

England is very different,
In every single way,
There's lots of rain and snow and wind
And the skies are often grey,
I wish you luck in Africa,
That all your dreams come true,
And when you read this poem,
Just how I've thought of you.

Claire Caskie (14)
Ripley St Thomas CE High School

Untitled

Jack was tired of being punched and kicked,
Sick of his face getting poked and flicked,
Today he would stand up to Chris the bully,
Chris was big and fat, his hair was woolly.

Chris came along, his fists clenched tight,
Jack got ready to put up a fight,
He gave Chris a hard bop on the nose,
Chris cried like a baby and told Miss Rose.

Jack was proud, he'd sorted Chris out,
But cried like a girl when he heard the shout,
He shook hands with Chris and they said sorry,
But what Jack meant was, 'Now you have to worry!'

Thomas Fleetwood (14)
Ripley St Thomas CE High School

Aids

Innocent little children
Born with the weight of death
No help,
No way of struggling free from its evil grip,
They have been passed down this devastating curse,
From the people who care for them the most.

More than 50% of the children are born with this madness,
It could be even more,
Our leaders couldn't give two hoots,
They're more wrapped up in war.

Every day death will be born
Yet killing in its thousands,
These children know no different
And will carry on this burden.

Jack Ireland (14)
Ripley St Thomas CE High School

My Life As A Chinese Orphan

Sitting silently tied to the chair,
There's nothing to do but sit and stare,
There are people around me but they don't care,
My life is just one great big nightmare.

There's no excitement, there's nothing to do,
'Hey lady over here, don't forget about me too,'
Who would do this, tell me who?
If you were here would you?

Now and again someone appears,
I'm waiting so patiently, 'Please come over here,'
I am so numb, I have no fear,
There's no emotion not even a tear.

Catherine Lund (14)
Ripley St Thomas CE High School

Conscience

Life is full of memories, the good, the bad and the worse,
Some have everything yet you have nothing,
In life you are at your most innocent as a child,
So why are you punished in such a cruel way?
You have done nothing wrong,
But yet you have no love, no care, no attention.

If people were to see what happens to you,
What you have to go through each and every day,
Would they listen to their conscience,
Or would they turn their backs as if there's nothing to see?

Do people see everything or just what they want to?
When they hear you cry, do they comfort you?
Do they heal your pain?
Do they stop your suffering
Or do they do nothing and leave you to die?

Jess Archer (14)
Ripley St Thomas CE High School

Children Of The World

Children of the world today,
Don't know how lucky they are,
Except for those in China who
Have had no life so far.

What would it feel like
To be in a room
With no one to talk to
And nothing to do?

Tied to a bed, so you cannot move about,
With all the layers on top of you,
No one can ever hear you shout,
And then after a lifetime of lying in the room,
You lie there motionless, never again to move.

Alex Johnson (14)
Ripley St Thomas CE High School

A Life Unlived

Being a girl, disabled, not perfect,
Sent away for a life unlived.
A baby wrapped in cloth and rags,
Numbed by the emptiness of the
Atmosphere around.

In a room alone they lay,
Shadowed with loneliness, hunger and thirst,
No cuddles today, tomorrow, next week,
Just an obligation to the carers they meet.

Isabel Burnside (14)
Ripley St Thomas CE High School

A Poem About Food!

My favourite food of all time,
I really have to say,
Is chocolate cake with hot fudge sauce,
I'd eat that any day!

But, then again, I do love chips,
Now, they really are delish!
Thick ones, thin ones, bring them on,
I'm sure that I will finish.

Ooh! Did I forget to mention this,
I love my Sunday roast,
And what I also really like,
Is bacon and beans on toast.

I love most kinds of junk food too,
But that's not all I eat,
I like the healthy foods as well,
Like rice and bits of meat.

I don't want a heart attack,
I don't want to be obese,
I'd rather live to see my grandkids grow,
So never eat too much grease!

Hannah Fletcher (13)
Rivington & Blackrod High School

Stomach Express

The mouth is open,
Ready for food,
The teeth are ready to churn and chew,
So watch out gullet,
And the stomach express.

Because food is ready, to come and compress,
For the intestines, it is ready to go,
It sets from the stomach, go, go, go,
If it gets delayed, the intestines are full,
And the rectum is shouting, 'Let me go.'
And we will not shout, if we exit,
As the stomach express finishes its journey
Ready for the next!

Ryan Harrison (14)
Rivington & Blackrod High School

Spring Flowers

Opened suddenly spring's begun
From the gentle touch of the welcome sun,
Hundreds of flowers lift their faces up,
Each with a surprise in its delicate cup.

Sweetly scented like a dream,
From fairyland they may seem,
Covering the land with warmth and glow,
Like a patchwork blanket, they would show.

As the flowers open wide,
Their scent is sweet and cannot hide,
They are everywhere to be seen,
Like a righteous country queen.

Rebecca Hannell (13)
Rivington & Blackrod High School

The Troublesome Land I Learned To Love

I've always wanted to be Welsh,
Or maybe even a Frenchman,
But a Celt I will remain
And hope these terrors end.

My land of fear,
Could come to an end,
The wrath intense; help is needed,
Or my land could die.

An image of war and terror
That spins around all our lives:
Children cry; parents weep,
But only exile calls them.

And so, my Ireland, I ask myself
It surely must be safe again.
But my hopes will remain forever
On this land of hopes and fears.

Tom O'Donnell (14)
Stonyhurst College

Time

Time ticks on inevitably,
It's as sure as the sunrise,
Tick-tock,
It's inevitable,
But what happens if it stops?

Will the people not age?
The flowers not die?
The winter not come?
Oh how boring that would be.

William O'Byrne (14)
Stonyhurst College

My Dog

My dog sits,
Rigid like a proud guard,
Her soft, but matted fur,
Stiffens when
I touch it.
Her soft, mysterious eyes gaze at me:
I often wonder what
She is thinking.
As I scratch her spiky neck,
She whimpers with glee.
And her musty smell,
Creeps up my nose.
Although it is not delightful
It makes me feel at ease and tranquil.
My dog's name is Tess.

Jack Wood (13)
Stonyhurst College

Losing Things

Things I'm always losing,
I never know where they are,
Under the bed,
Or in the shed,
It makes me swear in my head,
I never really know,
Where they seem to go,
I look for them forever,
But I will find them, never,
I search inside and out,
But they are never about,
Things I'm always losing,
I never know where they are.

Edward Johnson (13)
Stonyhurst College

The Unbreakable Bond

Our souls, they are together,
Though in bodies far apart.
I know you'll never leave me:
You're forever in my heart.

One night, at rest, you came to me:
A vision in the dark;
I shut my eyes, can't bear to see,
That face, which left its mark.

Someday I'll be in paradise,
Then meet you face to face.
I'll wrap my arms around you,
Take warmth from your embrace.

You always were the greatest,
My favourite one, through and through:
That day you were laid to rest,
My brother, life ceased without you.

Nicola Agius (16)
Stonyhurst College

I Hope No One Notices

I hope no one notices,
The mud on the door,
The dog hairs on the sofa,
And the drawing on the wall.

They'd better not notice,
The scratches on the car,
The broken window next door,
And the mess I've made so far!

If Mum finds out, she'll absolutely
Blow a fuse tonight,
When she knows who has done it,
She will die of fright!

Charlie Fogden (13)
Stonyhurst College

Grave

Beyond that yonder,
Through those irises entwined,
As if close friends, relatives.
But what is it, where is the truth, under that crippled tree,
Deep in eerie shadow,
A stone of significance,
A stone of peace.
How does the engraving relate,
The indentations like deep wounds, scars for all eternity.
Known to man what lies here,
Whose fault is it that nothing grows here?
The soils infertile, useless,
Yet useful:
To hold this stone,
For now.
For evermore.

Frances Warner (14)
Stonyhurst College

Winter

Winter is coming, it's in their eyes,
Crisp leaves falling from either side,
Slowly brown turns to white,
As the snow lies round about,
Autumn is dying, there's no escape,
Winds grow harsh, fires appear,
Animals hibernating everywhere,
Snow smells fresh upon the ground,
Air smells fresh all around,
A blanket of white fills the Earth,
Temperature falling like a new-winged bird,
I can almost taste it,
As it smells so good,
Make the most of it before it all goes.

Hugh Holt (13)
Stonyhurst College

The Fire Bird

As the last flame cried out,
And crackled with fear,
When nobody was about,
Who could see or hear.

While these ashes cooled,
They glowed a mysterious way,
For who would notice the mood,
Of where these ashes lay.

A spark of life, a single flame,
Come, more and more,
It's the Fire Bird to blame,
And then a fire did roar.

Rising from the fire,
Like a lost spirit, found,
Beating its wings hard, higher and higher,
Singing its song aloud, a wondrous sound.

Austin Culley (14)
Stonyhurst College

Sounds

Walking through the graveyard
Walking through the streets
Looking all around me
Surely sets off the creeps

Looking at the people quickly shuffling by
Running to the race dogs
Always catches eyes

People at the football match
Crowds and crowds around
Many people wonder what is with the sound.

Amy Townsend (14)
Stonyhurst College

Alone In The Night

All you can hear is silence,
Although that has no sound to be heard.
Yet now and then a cold wind blows
And the crisp leaves rustle like the sound of rain.
A bitter cold freezes the moon,
It makes the stars shiver
In their deep dark bed beyond.
Stillness is the scent hung sleepily on the air,
Like firewood and grass and the freshness of winter.
Darkness closes in on the air
And fills in each space with black shadows.
The sky above is a deep purple
Mixed heavily with grey.
Time has stood still in an eternity;
Never changing, like a dark secret, all is unknown.
It seems as though you are falling
In this darkness and stillness of the night,
And this stranger remains unnoticed,
Unrecognisable, insignificant in the dim gloom.

Vicky McNeill (14)
Stonyhurst College

Where Is She Now?

She wandered lonely, empty inside,
Forever searching for that warmth she longed for.
She watched helplessly when her life tumbled and crashed
As her walls of protection, slowly began to fade.
Surrounded by the tormenting fears,
There was no one to turn to.
She yearned for her life not to be forgotten,
Like a snowflake timidly vanishing in the snow.
But her life soon became meaningless,
Her name never to be heard,
For now only the wind,
Would know that she had ever stirred.

Gertrude Okello (14)
Stonyhurst College

Winter

The cold, frosty breeze swept in
As the wind charged over the surface of the Earth.
The autumn's harvest taken,
Outdoor life ceases
And the world is dormant,
For some it is miserable and a living Hell,
But others curl up into a protective shell.
This is a world where the fittest and the strongest survive.

Yet there is more beauty:
The snowflakes naturally created in geometrical shapes.
Mountains, which look overwhelming, exposed in the snow.
Trees towering, up to a certain point where the altitude is too high.
Evergreens, the only time of year where they give the impression
of being white.
Even in the most treacherous conditions, there is still beauty.

Marco Moreno (15)
Stonyhurst College

Miss Murphy's Tutees

Bang! Slam! Shut the door
'Where have you been?'
I started trembling on the floor
'Where are your lines?'
I begged, 'Please no more,
There you are Miss.'
With a smile on my face
I wish Old Murphy would get off my case
I sit down at my desk
But guess who runs in?
Little Miss Fullalove
Here we go again

Bang! Slam! Shut the door . . .

Bob Townsend (15)
Stonyhurst College

Snow

Snow is fun,
Snow is great,
In the summer I just can't wait.

Snow is wet,
Snow is white,
It glistens in the morning light.

Snow is light,
Snow is cold,
Into balls it can be rolled.

Snow is shallow,
Snow is deep,
Ploughers push it into heaps.

Snow is joy,
Snow is felt,
In the spring it will melt.

Patrick McFarlane (15)
Stonyhurst College

Tree

He lives with many others,
He is always motionless,
Always looking out.
He has a beard of
Thick moss,
A head of giant branches.
His legs are a mass of
Crisp, dirt-covered roots.
He is a shepherd
Of the forest
Until he silently ages
Away, never to
Be seen
Again.

Todd Robinson (13)
Stonyhurst College

The World, Which We Know And Love

The world, which we know and love,
Is slowly but surely coming to an end.
We wake up each day,
And try our best,
To ensure we deserve
Sweet, eternal rest.
And although what we don't know won't hurt us,
There are some things we just have to know.
Discrimination against our brethren,
No matter what the form,
Is a crime against humanity,
And is punishable with scorn.
Hatred and dishonesty
Can get you far in this world,
But if so, where does it get you
In the afterlife?
If we do not love each other,
There will be no sound rest.
Yet when we do,
We don't do it with our best.
Man would rather have all the money in the world
Than have a very good friend.
And I do not wonder why
When friends can be far worse enemies than those you strongly detest.
But I say to you my kindred
Do not overlook love and hate,
For this is what makes our lives
As human beings so great.

Onajite Emerhor (13)
Stonyhurst College

Shun!

'Shun! Right dress! Here!'
All this drill makes me feel
Depressed, annoyed, bored,
Until the under officers roared.

'Front, centre, rear,'
England, never fear.
The Stonyhurst Cadet Corps will save the world,
I can't wait until the first shot is hurled.

Out we go to have little fun,
Out we go into the sparkling sun,
Look at the light across the cloudless sky,
Whilst we are rifle-handling, all I can do is sigh.

The rifle is held up for all to see,
But to be honest, it's all beyond me,
Safety catch here and trigger there,
They think that I don't listen, it isn't fair.

Lying down in cow pats against imaginary foes,
Jumping over fences into mud, and off our platoon goes,
Running through nettles and crouching down again,
Think of the war, those poor men.

The pain is incredible and that's too small a word,
Nettle stings on hands and legs and a dirty, tired herd,
Surely it is over now but no more drill,
My anger is brewing up, I feel ready to kill.

Finally we are released from Hell and relief breaks loose,
We charge away like bulls but of course it's no use,
In one week's time it will all start again,
Once more in the chaos of the CCF den.

Anthony Satterthwaite (14)
Stonyhurst College

The Long Window

There on the island perched above the sea,
The hotel sat there peacefully,
Its west tower hanging over,
Off the shore of Dover.
There was a murder there some years ago,
Or should I say a slaughter,
For all the guests were killed that night,
By the owner's daughter.

There was a storm there some years ago,
The power went out,
And dark was all about,
Guests went missing here and there,
And one screamed like a bear.
I thought it was my daughter
About to join the dead,
I searched the hotel hour after hour,
Until I was followed and forced into the tower.

The handle turned and in pounced the murderer
But she tripped and hit the window,
Crashing into the long window
Falling to the rocks below.
As I peered down to the rocks
There on the dock,
The murderer,
My daughter . . .

Joshua McAllister (14)
Stonyhurst College

Little Tim Grew Up

When I was new,
He never put me down.
We were stuck with glue,
Always smiling, never a frown.

I went everywhere with him,
I was never out of sight.
Nothing ever seemed dim,
Not even the night.

He always visited the park,
And yes, I was there.
We played on till dark,
Till midnight to be fair.

But with time comes change,
Even if it's bad.
Everything was rearranged,
And I was left sad.

I was ignored for five years,
It got colder and colder.
My sorrows were drowned in tears,
Our childhood was over.

But one day he reappeared,
And took me to the park.
Little Tim had grown a beard,
How was I to know that I'd be *left* in the dark?

Matthew Richardson (15)
Stonyhurst College

Time

Time is a most wonderful and dreaded thing,
You can grow old, you can mature,
Because time is a most wonderful and dreaded thing,
But with time there is only one thing that is for sure,

Time will go on whether you want it to or not,
With time you will understand, that time has got to go on,
And with this gift I give to you, I am telling to you, I must say
We see the sunrise every morn and then it dies with the day,
But why is my question, when will time not go on?

If I knew I would tell to you,
But I am not that powerful,
I'm not that great, I don't even know
Who has the power to stop time?
Who has this power divine?

Guess what, I'm not telling
That is for you to find out,
I believe it is so, that the Lord alone
Has this power, He sings His voice and all is still,
But His voice is loud, to those who listen.

Adrian Riley (14)
Stonyhurst College

I Wish

I wish I could fly into the sky above just like a dove.
I wish I could live in the deep blue sea and explore all the
                                        hidden treasures.
I wish I could live in Neverland so I could be forever young and free.
I wish I could be a general going to war, giving orders to all my men.
I wish I could be a spy sneaking up on enemies, living way up high.
I wish I could teach, so I could help African children learn.
I wish I could be a policeman in New York, so I could help fight
                                        to keep peace.
Then I realise I wish only to be myself and myself only,
Because there is only one of me.

James Kennedy (15)
Stonyhurst College

Elements

Fire licks the place where it's contained,
Roaring, blazing, crackling,
Glowing with delight,
Destroying all it touches.

Water crashes against the rocks vigorously,
But then dies like a storm,
And flowing down a mountainside,
As a river or a stream.

Air blows the trees with strength and power,
But gently, silently, softly,
So you can hear the whisper
Of the elements.

Earth provides life and vitality,
A place for life to live,
Creating a world.

Rosanna Martin (14)
Stonyhurst College

The Competition

The tension is high but my spirits are low
Why oh why won't my nervousness go?
I look around and I see the crowd cheering
Why didn't I just stay in bed sleeping and dreaming?

All of a sudden I see in the corner of my eye
My family cheering, their hopes very high
I stand up straight my spirits become high
I thought I'd just give it a go and a try.

So I tried and tried and tried some more
I didn't stop trying till the final score
In the end I won, stood there staring and gazing
I couldn't believe I'd won, it was simply amazing.

Chuba Nwokedi (14)
Stonyhurst College

Where Is God?

Does God exist?
I guess we'll never know.
Does the Devil exist?
I guess we'll never know.
But one thing is for sure,
That when we find our true meaning in life,
We'll know that we were wrong to doubt.

People say that He made the Earth,
They say that He brought us here,
They say that He helps us,
Why then are people dying in war?

Why does He not help the sick,
Or why does He not answer your prayer
As you are bowing there?
You think to yourself, is this a waste of time
Or is this really worthwhile?

Why doesn't He come to me now?
Tell me that I am wrong!
Why will He not put the doubt out of my mind?
My guess is, I'll never know.

Alexander Ewart (15)
Stonyhurst College

Water

The sleek silence,
The rippling rapids,
The smooth stones,
The tranquil trees,
The slippery fish by the river.

Then the raging rapids,
Then the wild waterfall,
Then the thrashing thunder,
Then the sandy shore,
Then the slippery seaweed by the sea.

Luke Robinson (14)
Stonyhurst College

Earth

(Inspired by Gerard Manley Hopkins 1844-1889)

We dwell on the most fantastic object ever created,
Raised by human hands.
The huge orange sphere suspended strikingly
In the wide, open atmosphere.
The large ball blending in with the cool blue sky,
Until night when it crosses the sun
Then appears a large white ball gleaming and glistening
With the stars, like a father with his children.

The Earth is the greatest gift any man could desire.
The sun reflecting off the twinkling oceans,
A priceless jewel.
For this great gift we must thank our Father
Who lives up in Heaven.
The most rewarding seven days ever spent.
And given to us when we are born,
A priceless gift.

Daniel Church-Taylor (13)
Stonyhurst College

King Of The Sea

The sea is a dangerous place,
The waves rumble and grumble,
The wind howls; the rain hammers,
Who would dare to venture out there,
Other than the monster of the sea?
His long green neck, his shark-like fin,
His pointed teeth, his enormous body,
Make him king of the sea,
No one dares to enter his region,
Not even a legion,
He is king of the sea.

Chris Fitzgerald (14)
Stonyhurst College

Darkness And Pain

In the darkness there can only be an absence of light,
And in this darkness fear and hate take hold with true might.
For what hides in this pit of despair,
Demons and ghosts make a chaos which is rare.

Yet not all darkness is of shadow and blight,
It is also found in the mind, in the coolness of night.
For what springs from this field of madness and woe,
True evil rises and sheds its harvest to those down below.

Yet no man can see this field of insanity, the dead,
To look upon it is to join its lunacy and dread.
Those who join the graveyard of the lost,
Suffer great pain of deprivation and loss.

Many are those who join it, freely of heart,
And enjoy what is given to them, that which is naught.
For it takes much and returns nothing but pain,
What they lose is far greater than the little that they gain.

And still it goes on: the path and anguish,
They still laugh at the pain that they sow.
Yet they do not know what is funny,
For what is taken is forgotten and gone.

Edward Medwecki (15)
Stonyhurst College

The Harsh Reality Of War

Soldiers march with a spring in their step;
Their faces of pride, faces of patriotism, and faces of glee alike.
They are blinded from the truth;
Propaganda hides them from the harsh reality of war.

Young, ignorant men - even children - gradually discover
for themselves,
War is not a game, nor an adventure.
The disease, the vermin,
The wounds inflicted upon the enemy and received in turn -
what goes around, comes around.

What were once entertaining fireworks, become life-threatening,
exploding bombs.
Gunfire, once distant and powerless, is now the decider of life
and death.
Rain replaces sunshine, night replaces day.
Battlefields destroy nature.

Life and death.
Once an adventure for the men from the land of the young and free.
A chance to prove their country's power.
A chance to prove their country's worth.

A chance to travel,
A chance to defeat the enemy,
A chance to defeat the opposition,
Now a matter of life and death.

Benedict Burgess (15)
Stonyhurst College

The Athlete

As the athlete prepares for his race
His heart is beating at some pace.

He'd twist, turn and jump
As if it were remotely fun
He'd gallop and run right down the course
Like a beast and we were united as one.

Then he'd stood up on the podium
With a medal around my neck
But he's here in the kitchen
The floor a black and white check.

To run faster than the wind
To swim more smoothly than a fish
To be an Olympic athlete
Is his only wish.

Jack McGovern (15)
Stonyhurst College

The Shark

Backwards and forwards he patrols,
Looking for his prey.
Suddenly the sweet scent of blood!
In a flash, the scaly tail begins to beat,
Pumping, pumping, following the scent,
Before catching his prey.
The fish is speared in those needle-like teeth.
The shark has claimed another victim.

Sam Reed (13)
Stonyhurst College

Cloudy Mountain

Where there's clouds
And shower falls of rain
Where there's fog
So no one can see
Not even me
Cloudy mountain

Where there's many lakes
Ponds and seas
No one could swim
Not even me
Cloudy mountain

Where there's many people
No houses, no barns
Nowhere to stay
Not even for me
Cloudy mountain

Where there's only one mountain
There are many things
Many people, many waters
No one can go there
Not even me
It's fantasy
Cloudy mountain.

Molly Aylward (13)
Stonyhurst College

Freedom Of The Wolf

To be in the darkness of tall, sweet-smelling trees
To feel the wind and rain as you walk beneath the radiant sun
To have the warm rays of light give you the strength of the wind
To see all around your family, home and food.

The true meaning of freedom is with you always
When you hunt down the graceful deer and feel
His warm life-giving blood fill you with hope and power
To respect all living things and give thanks for their life.

Having no boundaries or cages and roam wherever
The elements can touch, choosing your own den; howling
Through the cold, frosty nights a howl that can never be tamed
And this truly is the freedom no other animal has:
The freedom of the wolf.

Isabel Howat (16)
Stonyhurst College

The Path

Venturing along the windy road
With a chill on my back and my fingers cold,
To a path I will come
To change the surroundings of my walk.

As I enter the path's mysterious world,
All my troubles suddenly disappear,
The deafening silence encaptures me,
The birds singing enlightens me,
The path's peace comes to an end.

Dan Layzell (14)
Stonyhurst College

To End All Wars

Face pressed hard against the side of the trench,
All night watching for them to come,
Ammunition checked, bayonet fixed,
Clenching the barrel of the gun.

Bodies to the left, bodies to the right,
And knowing they would not be the last,
Nobody knew who was going to be next,
To be killed in the next bomb blast.

The night was hard and stained with blood,
The terrible artilleries sound,
Morale? It's gone, their hearts have broken,
What with friends lying limp on the ground.

Then they finally came at morning's first light:
The shouts, the shots and then,
Our valiant brothers in arms shot back,
Mowing down at least half of them.

The enemy have broken, the cheers and cries,
Of our victorious lads,
The ladders came forth; the whistles were blown,
We are now on the counter-advance.

Then the shot came, the bullet with your name,
Penetrated your dirt-stained top,
Your legs collapsed under the strain,
You fall to an ultimate stop.

But you crawl your way to the edge of your ditch,
You're at the trench now; but you give out a cry,
Another shot has ripped through your eighteen-year-old leg,
And you fall into darkness, but why?

'Don't worry,' you said, the unnamed soldier,
As you gave out your last painful cry,
'I die for a cause, to end all wars!'
What an appalling way to die.

Joseph Curry (15)
Stonyhurst College

Chocolate

Chocolate, chocolate is my dream,
Cadbury's is the best.
Flake and Dream and Buttons too,
They are better than the rest.

I think that my dad is mad,
He says he does not like
'That lot'.
But I've decided that he's crackers,
And it's better just forgotten.

Emily Mullen (13)
Stonyhurst College

Friendship

Friends are there in times of need,
They're always there to do a good deed.
They're there for you when you're down and sad,
And they're always there to make you glad.

Friends make you happy, they make you smile,
Even if only for a little while.
Don't take advantage of your friends,
And if you do, always make amends.

Scarlett Thompson (16)
Stonyhurst College